PUTTING OUT THE
FIRE OF FEAR

Extinguish the Burning Issues in Your Life

Sharon Promislow

Enhanced
Learning

Enhanced Learning & Integration Inc.
#713 1489 Marine Drive,
West Vancouver, BC, Canada   V7T 1B8

National Library of Canada Cataloguing in Publication Data
Promislow, Sharon, 1943–
Putting out the fire of fear : extinguish the burning issues in your life

Includes bibliographical references and index.
ISBN 0-9681066-4-1

1. Stress management.   2. Stress (Psychology)
3. Self-care, Health I. Title.

RA785.P75 2002   155.9'042   C2002-900913-8

Cover Design by Cathrine Levan
Cover Photo credits Comstock, Inc. and Jeff Andrews
Layout by Matthew Fessenden
Photography by Jeff Andrews

Brain Gym, Brain Buttons, PACE ™, Hook-ups, Positive Points, The Rocker,
The Energizer, The Thinking Cap, Brain Organization Profiles, are all registered
trademarks and copyrights of the Educational Kinesiology Foundation,
and are used here with permission. For information write 1575 Spinnaker Drive,
Suite 204B, Ventura, CA   93001, or call 1-800-356-2109

Excerpts from this book previously appeared in *The Top 10 Stress Releasers*
© 1992, 1994, 1996, and *Making the Brain Body Connection*, © 1997,1998,1999

The procedures and techniques described in these materials are solely for educational
purposes. The author, and Enhanced Learning & Integration Inc. are not directly
or indirectly presenting any part of this work as a diagnosis or prescription for any
condition of any reader, nor making representation concerning the psychological or
physical effects for any of the ideas reported. Persons using these tests and correction
procedures do so entirely at their own risk.

DISTRIBUTED IN CANADA & U.S.A. BY GENERAL DISTRIBUTION SERVICES

Printed and Bound in Canada
First printing April, 2002

10   9   8   7   6   5   4   3   2   1

In loving memory of my parents
Anne and Sam Medzon,
who always encouraged me to follow my dreams.

To my husband Barry, and my family for their
unfailing support as I continue on this path.

Acknowledgments

First and foremost, thanks to my colleague Cathrine Levan, who kick-starts me out of neutral and into drive with her clarity, intent and encouragement. Her unfailing optimism, editing and computer skills were instrumental to this book actually getting done, cover and all. Thanks also go to Matthew Fessenden, whose layout (and ability to go without sleep) added immeasurably to this book.

Once again I must thank Dr. Wayne Topping, author of *Success Over Distress*, and my longtime mentor in stress management skills, for his generous help and editing. Thanks also to Dr. Paul and Gail Dennison, founders of the Educational Kinesiology Foundation, for their superb work in the area of learning through movement, and their insightful feedback on this project.

I am also deeply grateful to: Daniel Whiteside, Gordon Stokes and Candace Callaway, creators of Three In One Concepts, who brought new insight and power to the art of stress management and the self-responsibility model. I also thank Dr. John Thie who put down the roots of the specialized kinesiology tree by making laymen aware of what they could do to keep their bodies aligned, with his seminal work, *Touch For Health*.

I am additionally blessed with the support I have received through the years from Hushion House Publishing, Toronto. Thanks Bill, Jules and staff!

Thanks also to: Doris Bass, Barrie Bentley, Yvette Eastman, Blair McDonald, Stephanie Mogg, Robert Olma, Raleigh Philp, Sean Promislow, Edna Shapira, and Rick and Darlene Theissen, who all gave input at critical times. And also Elana, Judy and Aimee for great family dinners while I had no time to cook.

Last but not least, my thanks to my colleagues and students throughout the world who enrich me in friendship and professional insight.

Sharon Promislow

Your feedback is always welcome at
sharon@enhancedlearning.com

Contents

Preface   9
  The Current World Situation Feeds
    the Fire of Fear   9
  The Fear is Not the Fire   11
  What This Book Offers   13

SECTION 1 *The Fire Of Fear Ignites*
Introduction   15
  How We Lock Emotion Into the Physical Body   16
  The First Step to Putting Out the Fire of Fear   19
  What is Specialized Kinesiology?   21
  Activity Break   23

SECTION 2 *What Fires Are Flaring Up?*
The Pre-Check   27
  How to Measure Your Progress   28
  The Information Sandwich   33
  Stepping Into Stress   35
  What Fear Looks Like In Your Life   35
  What Ignites Your Fire of Fear   36
  Choose A Key Issue   37

Emotional, Mental and Behavioral Pre-Checks 38
The Physiological Pre-Checks 43
Interpreting Your Reaction to Stress 46

SECTION 3 *Fire Extinguishers:*
Reeducating Your Brain/Body Response 55

How to Use These Activities 56
Meet Some Energy Switches 58
How Will You Know if These Activities Help You? 61

1. Drink Water 62
2. Plug In For Balanced Energy 65
3. Cross Patterning 69
4. Polarized Breathing 76
5. Cook's Hook-ups 80
6. Emotional Stress Release 87
7. Eye Rotations 100
8. Anchoring 107
9. Be Sense-Able 110
10. Rub Out Tension & Headaches 115
11. Fear Tapping Points 119
12. Leg Muscle Release 124
13. Sacral Spinal Pump 126
14. The Energizer™ 128
15. Neck & Shoulder Release 130

SECTION 4 *Checking The Embers:*
The Post-Check 133

Post-Checking Your Reaction to Fear 134
Establishing a Maintenance Program 139

SECTION 5 *More Fire Fighting Equipment:*
The Muscle Check 141

Using a Muscle Check for Biofeedback 142

SECTION 6 *Other Burning Issues:*
Sources Of Stress In Your Everyday Life — 153

The Continuum of Well-Being — 155
What is Stress? — 156
A Closer Look at the Pot of Stress — 158
What is Your 'Achilles Heel'? — 161
A Quick Detour to Goal Setting — 163
The Three R's for Managing Stress — 165
How to Address Your Burning Issues — 168

SECTION 7 *Putting Out Everyday Fires:*
Applying the Model to Your Life — 169

Using Your Fire Extinguishers the Simplest Way — 170
The 'Quick Six' in Everyday Life — 171
A Simple Model to Work on Any Issue or Goal — 174
What Else Can You Do? — 190
In Conclusion — 194

SECTION 8 Addenda — 197

Stress From the Brain's Point of View — 198
The Nature of Ritual — 204
Working With Positive Statements
    and Affirmations — 208

SECTION 9 Reference — 211

Endnotes — 212
Educational Opportunities — 217
Bibliography — 223
Index — 228

Preface

The Current World Situation Feeds the Fire of Fear

Suicide bomber strikes in… Wall Street tumbles… Anthrax found in… Project deadline Thursday… Attacks throughout the night rage on in… Employment performance review next week… Ebola, AIDS, mad cow disease…

With each new onslaught, how do you react? Disbelief and denial? Anger and grief? A knot in your gut? Headache and pain? Fear that bad things could happen to you next?

Are you trapped into making future choices based on "what ifs" that limit your life options? Do you avoid enjoyable life activities (large crowds, etc.) or specific locations (heights, elevators, planes, etc.) because you fear your reaction?

Why you? Why now?

Worldwide terror and unrest are taking their toll on your brain and body, even if you are unaware of it. Whether you have experienced the trauma of terrorism and war first hand, or vicariously through news and images, your sense of personal and national safety has been shaken. The threat to the nation's economic security is a devastating blow either directly, or to others around you. The day to day demands of your personal life seem magnified when added to these new social realities, impacting your ability to cope.

> The body's classic stress response has evolved to help you survive an immediate crisis, but there are huge emotional, mental or physical repercussions if you lack effective long-term strategies to handle stress.

Each of us manifests stress differently. Stress symptoms can show up as edginess, withdrawal, anger, relationship challenges, loss of focus and concentration, or illness. The body's classic stress response has evolved to help you survive an immediate crisis, but there are huge emotional, mental or physical repercussions if you lack effective long-term strategies to handle stress. You can't afford to ignore how the brain/body connection works.

What is going on in there?

When you are under stress, your mind and body

send out orders that cause chemical and electrical changes in your body circuitry. Brain integration breaks down, and body messages get confused. Communication can break down between the left and right brain hemispheres, sensory organs can switch off involuntarily and energy can be prevented from reaching the areas of higher cortical reasoning. This means it becomes difficult to 'do' and 'think' at the same time and everything you do requires more effort.

The good news is that you can reeducate your body to react differently to things that used to trigger your stress response. This book will show you how to handle fear and other intense emotions, and how to attain a higher level of functioning, through the use of powerful techniques that actually create better neural pathways. You will learn how to thrive, rather than to simply survive, the demands of our current realities.

> The good news: We can reeducate our nervous system to react differently to the things that set off our stress response, allowing us new options.

The Fear is Not the Fire

What is Fear? Fear at its best is a conscious assessment of threat to our status quo, or even survival. It is perfectly rational to fear terrorism, anthrax, losing your job, the edge of a dangerous cliff, or a poisonous snake. At the heart of the concept of Fear is the belief that there is a real danger.

What then is the Fire? The Fire is the degree to which Fear triggers a reflexive, adrenaline pounding stress response, and a replay of old survival mechanisms. That is where perspective is lost, and Fear can become irrational. The Fire can be a sense of impending disaster locked into the psyche, coloring everything you feel, perceive or do.

Fear is not the enemy. We need it to help us make decisions to minimize unnecessary risk. We need to treat Fear as a messenger that alerts us to act appropriately in a potentially harmful situation. We need to make sure that the Fire doesn't make us overreact, or distrust our inner feelings. The purpose of this book is to teach you how to separate the Fear from the Fire—whenever, however and wherever it hits you: In a plane, office, boardroom, elevator; at home, the shopping mall, or on the street.

> Fear is rational; often our response to it is not. We don't need to eliminate fear—we need to disengage anxiety.

What this Book Offers

You will discover:

- How fear and intense emotion lock into your physical body (and how to unlock it)
- If you are harboring any symptoms of Posttraumatic Stress Disorder
- The modus operandi of stress and how to consciously identify where it lives in your body and your life
- A simple 3 step approach to handle stress when it hits

> The purpose of this book is to teach you how to separate the Fear from the Fire—whenever, however and wherever it hits you: In a plane, office, boardroom, elevator; at home the shopping mall, or on the street.

- The top techniques for reducing stress in any situation
- Why and how these activities work, plus variations to use unobtrusively in everyday life
- How to use our format to quickly identify and apply these principles to other stressful issues in your life

This book is deliberately written for laypeople, although good references are provided for those who wish further substantiation. When under stress the last thing you need is a scholarly analysis of its effects. Stress has shut down your avenues to easeful processing and understanding, and set in action a chemical stew designed for your immediate survival, not intellectual discourse. The Activities in *Putting Out the Fire of Fear* are meant to be experienced with all your senses. The book has been laid out specifically as a workbook to help you absorb these techniques into your life more effectively. So don't just read the book: Do it!

Take it easy and be self responsible

You will be introduced to some gentle body movements designed to develop neural connections to energize you and improve the communication between your brain and body. Just remember: The only expert on you is you, and there should never be any discomfort as you do these activities. Do them only to the extent they are comfortable, and be congruent with the advice of your licensed medical practitioner. Small movements can activate the circuits as effectively as big ones.

> Disengage yourself from old established survival patterns and establish new neural pathways to more productive behaviors and feelings.

The activities will help you to disengage yourself from your old established survival patterns (historically triggered by fear), and to establish new neural pathways to more productive behaviors and feelings. Simply expressed, you will put out the fire of fear.

SECTION 1

THE FIRE OF FEAR IGNITES

Introduction

THE FIRE OF FEAR IGNITES
Introduction

How We Lock Emotion Into the Physical Body

How we feel, how we think and how we behave are integrally fused with our physical being. In order to handle strong negative emotions like fear, we must understand this link, and how it impacts our perception of life events.[1]

Our emotional experience consists of a feeling, a physiological and a behavioral response. Everyone talks about the power of positive thinking. We all know that a change in how you feel and think leads to changes in your body state and how you behave. Add to that the power of positive action, and the power of positive body states. Change your behavior, and your emotions and your physiology will change—body chemistry, neurology, posture and more. Equally, reeducating your physiology has the power to change your emotional and behavioral states. Make a change in any one of the states, and it ripples down to the other two, then cascades down into your perceptual filter of the world.[2]

When we experience an event, we color it with our own meaning and emotion as part of our reaction. For example; you are walking down the street and a car backfires. The inbred startle reflex is triggered and the brain must interpret the alert—"Am I in danger?" In the past we might have let it go, and returned to neutral body chemistry. Today we have been cautioned to be 'on guard', so we react: "Could it be a gun? Is it an attack?" and all the neural circuits firing at the time of the backfire—the exact position of your body, the muscles that are being used, the direction of your eyes and especially the emotions you feel—become fused into a circuit of cellular memory. From that moment on, each time you fire off any part of that

> All the neural circuits firing at the time of the stressful event become fused into a circuit of cellular memory.

circuit you will fire off the whole set of reactions that was part of your survival response in that first moment. When you later use the same muscle sequence, look in the same direction, experience a similar event, or feel the same emotion, you will trigger the whole fused set. You then can't figure out why suddenly you feel jumpy, have a change of mood, cannot think clearly or have a pain in your back. What you are experiencing is a "stuck circuit lock".

We can express it as a simple formula[3]:

Event + Perception + Intense Emotion = Stuck Circuit Lock

We are not simply reacting to stress in the moment. We are triggering cellular memory of similar past experiences that are overlaid on the same brain and body receptor sites. This is how memory works: We are the sum total of all our life experiences (good and bad), more deeply etching our past reactive behavior patterns into brain/body circuitry with each repetition of our response.[4]

> To a stressed system, survival is the bottom line, and changes to the way you respond to stressful situations are seen as potentially harmful.

To a stressed system, survival (any way you can get it) is the bottom line, and changes in the way you respond to stressful situations are seen as potentially harmful. Under stress our body/brain feels it is serving us best by reminding us of similar situations in the past which we have lived through. We have survived to this moment, even if we are dysfunctional. Our brain considers this a great success, so it orders us to do and feel more of the same. You will learn how to identify these old 'stuck circuit locks' and how to release them with simple and specific brain/body balancers.

The First Step to Putting Out the Fire of Fear

The first half of *Putting Out the Fire of Fear* has a special focus. It allows you to explore privately and safely, whether you are experiencing any specific symptoms of Posttraumatic Stress Disorder or another anxiety disorder. These symptoms often do not show up for months or years after a causative trauma, and are often ignored until there is an escalation of the problem. It's foolish to 'tough it out' if your stress resilience has been stretched to a breaking point. Why pay a high personal cost, when it can be avoided with some basic understanding of how your brain and body work, and a few minutes of easy self-care.

> Explore privately and safely, whether you are experiencing any specific symptoms of Posttraumatic Stress Disorder or another anxiety disorder. These symptoms often do not show up for months or years after a causative trauma

Posttraumatic Stress Disorder

Severe Posttraumatic Stress Disorder (PTSD) is uncommon, but very real and serious. It is diagnosed when exposure to an unexpected and/or shattering event continues to have a serious negative effect on a person long after the danger has passed, and equilibrium should have been restored to the nervous system. He/she becomes trapped into a constant replay of stress reactions triggered by the original event. The trauma remains ever present.

However, our 'new reality' is that we have all been warned to remain constantly vigilant and alert to possible threats to our safety, and even to help foil additional attacks. As we will explore later, this places us in an 'Alarm' survival state that triggers many emotional, physiological and mental responses that mirror symptoms of PTSD.

> Being vigilant places us in an 'Alarm' survival state that triggers many emotional, physiological and mental responses that mirror symptoms of Posttraumatic Stress Disorder (PTSD).

At the same time we have been called upon to resist becoming disheartened, which is the goal of those who attack our way of life. How can we get back to business as usual, in the face of nameless threat? How can we keep 'on guard' and be relaxed at the same time? Vigilance can be debilitating, or it can take the form of relaxed alertness, allowing us to move through our environment with assurance, a sense of personal safety and self-control.

This book is not intended as a substitute for the professional mental health support needed by those experiencing serious PTSD and mental illness. For most of us, the symptoms evaluated in Section 2 are simply indicators of chronic stress. This book will help you to identify which stressors are at play in your life, to notice the intensity of their impact, and to re-evaluate the positive effects of adopting the powerful strategies presented herein.

> We will teach you to use "matter over mind" as well as "mind over matter" techniques. You will learn "why", "where" and "how" to activate hidden switches and buttons on the human body.

What is Specialized Kinesiology?

Kinesiology is defined as the study of the body in movement. Specialized Kinesiology is the field that looks at how muscles, movement and posture are affected by emotional, mental and physical factors in our life and vice versa. This field of study synthesizes principles and techniques from Applied Kinesiology, acupressure, energy theory, current brain research, stress management, Neuro Linguistic Programming, chiropractic and body work, into an open-ended energy-based model for reeducating the body's neural response to stress.[5]

Specialized Kinesiologists look for energy and functional blockage within the body systems themselves, and use this information to pinpoint where improvement is needed. Specialized Kinesiologists concentrate exclusively on restoring natural energy flow and movement to the body, and releasing any blockages with gentle body/muscle reeducation.

You are about to learn "why", "where" and "how" to activate many of the switches and buttons on the human body. These "buttons and switches" all work to release stuck energy circuits and faulty communication between the brain and the body. Using these energy switches can restore the normal flow of energy and brain/body messaging, at the same time stimulating other important body systems—the lymphatic system, the neurovascular system, our central nervous system to name but a few.

> The reeducation activities in this book have been used successfully for over 28 years in the education, professional counseling and wellness sectors.

The reeducation activities in this book have been chosen because of their simplicity and practicality. Drawn from the whole field of Specialized Kinesiology, they have been used successfully for over 28 years in the educational, professional counseling and wellness sectors. These activities can profoundly affect brain function, and more than that, affect change in the cellular response of the body as well.

In Summary: We will identify the locks—both obvious and subtle—that underlie our energy blocks arising from fear and stress. Once identified, we will use energy switches and gentle processes to unlock our emotion, perception and physical reaction to the original event. We will then confirm that a change has taken place in how we manage our resources in the face of stress and fear. Now let's get on to identifying those locks.

First, an Activity Break

Make no mistake—you will be triggering the stress response as you identify and assess the impact of stress on your life. Therefore, you have a choice. I invite you to feel free to work through the book from front to back at your own pace, or to break away at any time to benefit from our Fire Extinguishers.

> Feel free to work through the book from front to back at your own pace, or to break away at any time to benefit from our Fire Extinguishers.

In fact, to help put you in the calm, balanced energy state to get the most from this book, why not briefly experience three activities right now? You will explore them in more depth later.

A MENTAL/ELECTROMAGNETIC BALANCER: Drink Water (page 62)

Get out your water bottle. Proper hydration is essential for good health on many levels. Relating to brain/body communication, water provides the medium necessary for optimum messaging throughout the brain/body. It increases energy, improves concentration and academic skills. Water is the number one stress releaser, so have a glass of water now.

- *Daily: One 10 oz. glass for every 30 lbs of body weight OR one 250 ml glass for every 10 kg of body weight*

- *Plus: 1 glass for each cup of coffee or caffeinated drink*

- *Plus: 2 glasses for every alcoholic drink*

- *More if you are exercising heavily or under stress*

A PHYSICAL AND BRAIN INTEGRATION BALANCER: Cross Patterning (page 69)

Use this technique when you find it hard to "do" and "think" at the same time. Cross Patterning activates communication between the two brain hemispheres and the whole body.

1. *Do a set of cross march, moving right arm to touch the left knee, then the left arm to touch the right knee, very deliberately and slowly.*

2. *Switch to one-sided march (same-sided hand and leg move together, like a puppet on a string) also very deliberately and slowly.*

3. *Alternate sets 6 or 7 times.*

4. *Always finish on the cross march.*

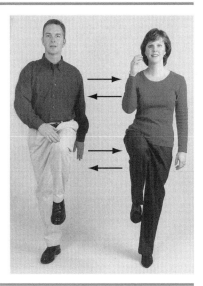

AN EMOTIONAL BALANCER:
Emotional Stress Release (page 87)

Whenever you feel under pressure, hurt or shocked, take the emotional edge off by holding your Emotional Stress Release (ESR) Points. Put your fingertips over your forehead, above your eyebrows. Keep them there while you think through your problem, or talk it out. Holding your ESR points keeps blood in your forebrain for clearer planning and thinking.

1. *Hold your forehead lightly with your fingertips and tug up slightly.*

2. *Think through any stressful event, past, present or future.*

Take a deep breath, and notice if you already feel calmer and more in control. This conscious noticing of any difference in reaction will allow the brain to truly register that you now enjoy a higher baseline of integration and functioning, and will help anchor in the improvement.

We are now ready to explore how the issue of fear and anxiety affects us. Take a deep breath, and let's begin.

SECTION 2

WHAT FIRES ARE FLARING UP?

The Pre-Check

WHAT FIRES ARE FLARING UP?
The Pre-Check

The first step is to understand how your brain and body operate—how our species instinctively reacts for bottom-line survival. Once you have consciously learned to identify your stress reactions, you will be ready to reeducate your neural responses to those old stimuli, and to experience better solutions and actions.

How to Measure Your Progress

How will you know which activities are most effective for you? Rather than using expensive, high tech biofeedback equipment, we advocate a simple paste-on Biodot, and two no-cost, effective techniques used extensively in Specialized Kinesiology. We will use these techniques to pre-check our brain/body's reaction to stress, and later to measure an improvement.

> We advocate three effective, simple biofeedback techniques to measure our brain/body's reaction to stress: Biodots, Muscle Checking, and Noticing.

1. **Biodots:** Using the same principle as the 'mood ring', small paste-on Biodots change color from black (stressed) to green/blue (relaxed yet alert) to lavender (trance, bliss state). Many health professionals recommend Biodots to their clients to help them get constant thermal biofeedback on their physiological response to stress. See page 238 for more information.

2) **Muscle Checking:** Muscle Checking is a superb means for providing biofeedback from the brain and central nervous system by testing the integrity of muscle strength and balance. Muscles physically weaken or tense under any kind of stress (mental, emotional, physical), and will return to normal again when the stress is resolved. When we use Muscle Checking, we are not measuring the strength of a muscle itself, but rather evaluating the nervous system that controls the muscle's function.

If you know how to Muscle Check, feel free to use this skill in the evaluations that follow; if not and you wish to learn how, consult the Educational Opportunities section on page 217–222 to be referred to a practitioner or an instructor near you.[6]

3) **Noticing:** Noticing is an effective means of biofeedback that helps us recognize our current mental, physical and emotional state. It calls for us to momentarily be still and to focus inward. Noticing is an in-depth self-awareness that is not self-conscious, which by definition makes you define yourself by how you perceive others are seeing and judging you. Instead, it is an objective internal self- monitoring of how you are functioning in the current moment. How do your muscles feel? Do you have any pain? Are your eyes and ears working fully? With Noticing we use our awareness to discern sub-optimal states of functioning in our posture, muscle tension, breathing patterns and sensory activity, as well as emotional and mental functioning. We will use a simple Noticing process at every stage of this book to give you a window into your present internal states. As a first step you will do an in-depth Noticing of how you feel and function when you are relaxed.

> Noticing is an effective means of biofeedback that gives us a window into our present internal states.

Noticing How Your Body Acts and Reacts When You Are Relaxed

Take a minute to do the following Noticing activity. Stand comfortably and imagine yourself in a relaxing situation (e.g. a beach in Hawaii). Now objectively notice your brain/body states, remembering there are no rights or wrongs, just what is. This exercise will give you a relaxed baseline against which you can later measure your body's reaction to stress. Jot down your findings.

Notice your posture in relation to the floor. (e.g. upright, swaying forward, backwards or sideways)

_____

Notice any tension, pain or weakness in your body. Where is it? (e.g. legs, back, shoulders, neck, stomach, chest, throat, jaw)

_____

Notice the pace of your heartbeat—slow and steady, or fast.

_____

Notice the pace and depth of your breathing.

_____

Notice if your mouth is moist or dry.

_____

Notice your body temperature. Do some parts of your body feel warm, and others cool?

_____

Notice your emotional state. How are you feeling? Excited, happy, sad, tense, motivated, withdrawn, etc.

_____

Notice your mental state. Can you think clearly or are you confused?

_____

Look at an object straight ahead. Is it clear or blurry?

_____

Listen to a sound in the room. Is it tinny or resonant? Are you hearing equally through both ears?

_____

Lift your straight arms up 30° in front of your body. Is that easy or does it take effort?

_____

Hold your arms there for 30 seconds. Is it easy or difficult?

_____

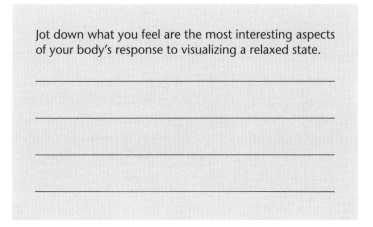

Jot down what you feel are the most interesting aspects of your body's response to visualizing a relaxed state.

_____

_____

_____

_____

Now that you have experienced our Noticing procedure, you might wonder how we are going to use it. We use Noticing to create an Information Sandwich:

The Information Sandwich

The top slice of the sandwich: First we Pre-Check how we feel and are functioning, keeping a specific goal or stressor in mind. We observe how effectively we are currently performing, and objectively recognize our current reaction patterns and functional blockages. The checklists that follow will trigger all your key issues, and give you a clear understanding of the physiological as well as the emotional and mental markers you have been experiencing as a result of stress. This Pre-Check will allow you to notice how you feel and function before using the Stress Releasers, giving you a baseline against which you can measure later improvement.

The filling: We then do a number of integrating targeted activities—'Fire Extinguishers'—to release the blockages created by stress in our brain/body system. Each activity has been chosen for its ability to balance the body in a specific way. Use them until a shift is felt in your state.

The bottom slice: The Post-Check—We think again of our goal/stressor, or go back to the activity that was previously performed less than optimally. We repeat the Noticing process to assess our improvements in functioning. If we have improved enough, our work is complete. If we are not yet satisfied, we simply repeat the balancing activities or add new ones until we achieve our desired level of enhanced performance. It's simple and pragmatic: We notice whether we feel better, if things feel easier, or if we are functioning more effectively.

THE INFORMATION SANDWICH

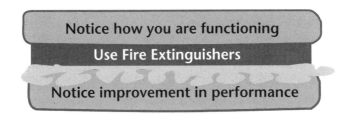

Notice how you are functioning

Use Fire Extinguishers

Notice improvement in performance

Stepping Into Stress

Now it's time to start activating the stress reactions you will be neutralizing as we move through the education process in this book. Don't be discouraged if it doesn't feel good to bring them into conscious awareness. That's the purpose—to pinpoint those reactions, so we can work on eradicating non-serving responses!

If at any point you are feeling too anxious to continue the Pre-Check, go back to pages 24–26 to do the three Activities you have already experienced, or jump forward to the next section to learn a few more Fire Extinguishers, returning here when you feel ready.

What Fear Looks Like in Your Life

First you will take a close look at Emotional, Mental and Behavioral Pre-Checks—written checklists that you will consciously evaluate. Then you will once again do the Noticing process, for more subtle and subconscious physiological pre-checks triggered by delving into stressful issues.

You will be activating stress circuits. Feel free to jump ahead into the Fire Extinguishers (page 62) at any point, until calm is restored.

BRAINSTORM: What Ignites Your Fire of Fear?

- ○ Flying
- ○ Bioterrorism (anthrax, smallpox, etc.)
- ○ Opening the mail
- ○ Nuclear weapons
- ○ War
- ○ Public places
- ○ Suicide bombers
- ○ Revenge
- ○ Foreigners
- ○ Economic downturn
- ○ Drive-by shootings
- ○ Drug wars
- ○ Phobias
- ○ Disease (AIDS, cancer, ebola, etc

Write down any key images, experiences or phobias that immediately spring to mind, causing you fear or distress.

_____

_____

_____

_____

Choose A Key Issue

Choose one of the above stressors as your sample burning issue to defuse as you work through this book. Your reaction to this issue at the end of the book will more clearly allow you to notice the difference in your brain/body response as a result of the concepts and activities presented. Think of your issue in great detail, to trigger any stuck circuit locks. Move your body in a 30 second roleplay of what you would do when first confronted with the stressor as a reality.[7] If you change your mind a little later as to what your true key issue is, just come back to this page and change your entry, or make a note that you will deal with that issue next.

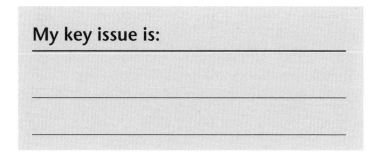

My key issue is:

1. Emotional, Mental and Behavioral Pre-Checks

Take a few minutes to read through the lists of behaviors that follow. The intent of the lists is not to label yourself with a psychological condition. It is simply to allow your brain to register where you should be looking for improvements as you begin experiencing the Fire Extinguishers taught in the next section. The more non-serving patterns you consciously identify, the more your brain can begin to self-correct.

> What the brain consciously identifies as relevant, it's inclined to correct, so the more symptoms you consciously identify, the more benefit you will experience.

Current brain research shows that what we imagine causes virtually the same brain firing pattern as actual experience. It is not unusual for people who have experienced terror only through news and pictures, to echo some of the symptoms of real life disaster victims. The images seen, the warnings heard, make all vulnerable to the possibility of fear and anxiety.

In some cases symptoms may appear months or years after the traumatic event. Be aware that the anniversary of the trauma is a particularly vulnerable date for triggering symptoms. There are three categories of symptoms that professionals consider as indicators of Posttraumatic Stress Disorder—stress triggered by a specific event. These are:

1) recurrent memories of the event, 2) changes in sleeping patterns and/or increased alertness, and 3) avoidance and emotional numbing[8].

Following these lists I invite you to evaluate some common stress-related physical and behavioral symptoms you may have experienced.

At the end of this section we will interpret your findings in light of the stress response.

Do Any of These Apply to You?

Rate each imbalance on a sliding scale between 0 and 10, and record what you notice.

Recurring Memories

	no impact			moderate			overwhelming			
Flashbacks—feeling like the event is happening all over again	0 1 2 3 4 5 6 7 8 9 10									
Strong mental and emotional pain when reminded of the event	0 1 2 3 4 5 6 7 8 9 10									
Nightmares or repetitive bad dreams	0 1 2 3 4 5 6 7 8 9 10									

Hyperarousal or Alarm

	no impact			moderate			overwhelming			
Difficulty falling or staying asleep	0 1 2 3 4 5 6 7 8 9 10									
Becoming overly startled by common noises or someone unexpectedly coming up to you from behind	0 1 2 3 4 5 6 7 8 9 10									

	no impact				moderate			overwhelming		
Being constantly "on alert" for danger	0	1	2	3	4	5	6	7	8	9	10
Unexplained fear, agitation or irritability	0	1	2	3	4	5	6	7	8	9	10
Feeling shaky, shortness of breath, breaking out in a cold sweat or irregular heartbeat when talking/ thinking about the event	0	1	2	3	4	5	6	7	8	9	10
An overwhelming feeling of upset triggered by a sight, smell, taste, sound or touch	0	1	2	3	4	5	6	7	8	9	10
Trouble controlling emotions—sudden outbursts of anxiety, anger, or sadness	0	1	2	3	4	5	6	7	8	9	10
Defiant/hard to discipline	0	1	2	3	4	5	6	7	8	9	10

Avoidance And Numbing

	no impact				moderate			overwhelming		
Emotionally numb and detached	0	1	2	3	4	5	6	7	8	9	10
Difficulty feeling love or any strong emotion	0	1	2	3	4	5	6	7	8	9	10
Feeling disconnected from events and people, a sense of unreality	0	1	2	3	4	5	6	7	8	9	10
Avoiding thinking or talking about the event	0	1	2	3	4	5	6	7	8	9	10
Avoiding activities, places, or people that are reminders of the event	0	1	2	3	4	5	6	7	8	9	10
Forgetting important details about the traumatic event	0	1	2	3	4	5	6	7	8	9	10
Losing interest in activities that were previously enjoyed	0	1	2	3	4	5	6	7	8	9	10

	no impact				moderate				overwhelming	
Believing that important goals— marriage, parenthood, or growing older— cannot be attained	0	1	2	3	4	5	6	7	8	9	10
'Self-medicating' with alcohol and/or drugs	0	1	2	3	4	5	6	7	8	9	10
Unable to focus in the moment— constantly daydreaming	0	1	2	3	4	5	6	7	8	9	10
Unable to remember common information, i.e., name, address, telephone number, etc.	0	1	2	3	4	5	6	7	8	9	10
Difficulty concentrating or thinking clearly	0	1	2	3	4	5	6	7	8	9	10
Difficulty making decisions	0	1	2	3	4	5	6	7	8	9	10
Self-harming, by cutting, burning, piercing, etc.	0	1	2	3	4	5	6	7	8	9	10

Common physical reactions may include:

	no impact				moderate				overwhelming	
Sudden onset of allergies	0	1	2	3	4	5	6	7	8	9	10
Stomach pains, constipation/diarrhea	0	1	2	3	4	5	6	7	8	9	10
Shakiness, chills, racing heart, when seeing reminders of the event	0	1	2	3	4	5	6	7	8	9	10
Respiratory problems	0	1	2	3	4	5	6	7	8	9	10
Headaches	0	1	2	3	4	5	6	7	8	9	10
Muscle cramps or aches	0	1	2	3	4	5	6	7	8	9	10
Sudden loss of bladder control	0	1	2	3	4	5	6	7	8	9	10
Low back pain	0	1	2	3	4	5	6	7	8	9	10

	no impact				moderate				overwhelming		
Cardiovascular problems	0	1	2	3	4	5	6	7	8	9	10
Anxiety disorder	0	1	2	3	4	5	6	7	8	9	10
Depression	0	1	2	3	4	5	6	7	8	9	10

More behavioral symptoms may include:

	no impact				moderate				overwhelming		
Accident prone	0	1	2	3	4	5	6	7	8	9	10
Clumsy	0	1	2	3	4	5	6	7	8	9	10
Loss of confidence	0	1	2	3	4	5	6	7	8	9	10
Inability to complete projects	0	1	2	3	4	5	6	7	8	9	10
Moody	0	1	2	3	4	5	6	7	8	9	10
Over-active	0	1	2	3	4	5	6	7	8	9	10
Poor reading comprehension	0	1	2	3	4	5	6	7	8	9	10
Restless/fidgety	0	1	2	3	4	5	6	7	8	9	10
Rub eyes a lot	0	1	2	3	4	5	6	7	8	9	10
Overly sensitive	0	1	2	3	4	5	6	7	8	9	10
Talk too much	0	1	2	3	4	5	6	7	8	9	10
Unpredictable	0	1	2	3	4	5	6	7	8	9	10

Now that you have activated countless 'stuck circuit locks' as you evaluated these reactions to stress, let's see how it has impacted your current body state. Stand up!

2. The Physiological Pre-Checks

Take a minute to do the following insight activity to see what the effect has been on your body systems. Record what you notice. A full explanation will immediately follow. Your body is constantly providing an external picture of your internal process.

Noticing How Your Body Acts And Reacts Under Stress

Keeping in mind your key issue, do this Noticing process. Stand comfortably and objectively Notice your body responses.

Notice your posture in relation to the floor. (e.g. upright, swaying forward, backwards or sideways)

_____

Notice any tension, pain or weakness in your body. Where is it? (e.g. legs, back, shoulders, neck, stomach, chest, throat, jaw)

_____

Notice the pace of your heartbeat—slow and steady, or fast.

_____

Notice the pace and depth of your breathing.

_____

Notice if your mouth is moist or dry.

_____

Notice your body temperature. Do some parts of your body feel warm, and others cool?

_____

Notice your emotional state. How are you feeling? Excited, happy, sad, tense, motivated, withdrawn, etc.

_____

Notice your mental state. Can you think clearly or are you confused?

_____

Look at an object straight ahead. Is it clear or blurry?

_____

Listen to a sound in the room. Is it tinny or resonant? Are you hearing equally through both ears?

_____

Lift your straight arms up 30° in front of your body. Is that easy or does it take effort?

_____

Hold your arms there for 30 seconds. Is it easy or difficult?

_____

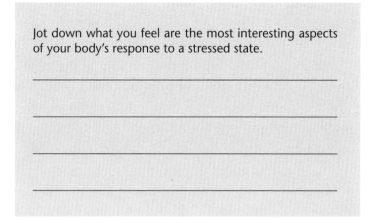

Jot down what you feel are the most interesting aspects of your body's response to a stressed state.

_____

_____

_____

_____

Compare these results with your relaxed baseline responses already recorded on pages 31–33 and note the key differences. These noticed states become our key yardstick against which we can measure the efficacy of the activities we are going to use to reeducate our reaction to stress. It is recommended you return to these preliminary evaluations to notice improvements in how you feel and function both immediately upon completion of the book, and again in the weeks to come. A myriad of symptoms may be occurring as a simple result of too much stress, period. Handle the stress, and don't be surprised if many of them disappear.

You can get even more specific with pre-checks by determining your personal Brain Organization Profile—eye, ear, hand and other dominances[9]. For our purposes here, it is enough to know that as soon as we are stressed, communication breaks down between the right and left sides of the brain, and we lose up to 70% of our non-dominant functioning. We revert to preset patterns of perception and behavior that may not serve us to our highest benefit. These set patterns become historical once you start using the stress releasers in this book. You will once again have access, even under stress, to the wisdom of your whole brain and all your senses.

Interpreting Your Reaction to Stress

We will now interpret the meaning of the body signals you noticed in the previous insight activities.

The Noticing exercise you did on pages 43–45 gave you information on your body's reaction to stress. In order to understand the classic stress response, we have to be aware of its relationship to health and well-being. Remember, the stress response evolved to help us survive a threat, such as when we are under physical attack. We are hard wired to react to threat for our survival (alarm stage), and to resolve that stress, restoring balance to our system (response stage). The stress response does not serve us if we are being asked to consider, but not act upon, a difficult situation.

New ideas and choices (a front brain activity) are impossible while we are trapped in our back-brained, reactive survival patterns.

If we are able to respond actively to a stressor or stressful situation, neutralize it and restore ourselves, there is little long-term ill effect. However, we often do not act, because of lack of awareness and/or inadequate coping skills. This will inevitably lead to the overwhelm stage, where we have exhausted our resources, and ongoing symptoms occur. Major learning, health and emotional disorders can result if stress is not appropriately handled, and the early signs are there before major problems develop.

> If we are able to respond actively to a stressful situation, there is little long-term effect.

So let's compare and interpret what you noticed in your insight activities with the signals of the classic stress response, so you can recognize them for what they are.

1. Alarm Stage Signals

As mentioned, the classic stress response has been wired into our species for our survival. When we are confronted with a perceived threat, blood immediately goes to the back, 'fight, flight or freeze' survival centers, cutting off flow to the front lobes of the brain. This is fitting, as primitive man had to react instantly and fight or flee for survival. He didn't have time to consider additional intellectual options that front-brained activity would provide.

Blood also leaves the digestive centers and goes to the large skeletal muscles to give him maximum strength. Good idea, since what does digestion matter if you might be dead in a few minutes? We have stories, even today, of a petite woman picking up a car to rescue a hurt child. This feat would be impossible without the adrenaline rush that goes along with stress, with increased blood flow to the large skeletal muscles and decreased blood flow to the rational front brain (which might tell her it's an impossible task).

> Alarm Stage: Blood leaves front brain and digestion, and goes immediately to back brain survival centers, and to arms and legs for 'fight or flight'.

Now let's compare the classic stress response to your own experience. Look back for a moment to your Noticing exercise on pages 43–45. Here is how the body is physiologically reacting to the initial alarm stage of stress.

Did you notice: *A change in the way you felt? Did your body begin to sway forward or back, left or right?* Swaying can indicate an over focused or under focused state, as does a feeling of hyper alertness versus spaciness.

Did you notice: *Tension or pain in your legs, back, shoulders, neck or jaw?* Muscles tense up preparing us for the fight/flight response, (the classic tendon/ guard response) so we can fight off the aggressor, or run out of harm's way. However, if we don't respond appropriately, or just freeze instead, these same tense muscles result in the chronic pain (particularly back, shoulder, neck and headache) so often associated with stress.

Did you notice: A sense of anger? A red, warm face? Along with tight muscles, the fight/anger response is also reflected in blood rushing to the upper body, hands and face.

Did you notice: Your face going white and clammy? A sense of dreaming, terror, or weakness? The flight/fear response moves blood from the head and upper body and goes to the legs for running.

The classic tendon/guard reflex causes the chronic tension and pain (particularly of the back, shoulders and neck) so often associated with stress.

Did you notice: A knot or pain in your stomach or gut? Digestive problems ensue as the blood is diverted from the digestive system as a result of emergency alert orders being sent out by the adrenal system.

Did you notice: A dry mouth? Find it hard to swallow? This is due to the reduced production of digestive enzyme (saliva) in the mouth. It's the reason we need a glass of water when giving a stressful speech. This symptom was used in ancient China as a lie detector test: If you couldn't swallow a mouthful of dry rice after giving an answer, you were lying.

Did you notice: *A change in your heart rate?* Tension in your chest? Were you holding your breath, or breathing more quickly? The brain needs more oxygen under stress, so the heart and lungs start working double time. With shock, we sometimes forget to breathe and end up being light-headed.

Did you notice: *A difference in your vision?* Your pupils dilate to increase peripheral vision for heightened awareness of possible attackers. Not so great today if you are preparing for a presentation, and read everything three times with no focus or comprehension!

> Pupils dilate to increase peripheral vision for heightened awareness of possible attackers. Not so great if you are preparing for a presentation, and read everything three times with no focus or comprehension!

Did you notice: *A difference in your hearing or comprehension?* When we don't feel safe, we don't filter out sound, for fear of missing an attack. Concentration and the ability to focus and understand using your higher brain functions are impaired.

Other Physiological Reactions That Impact Well-Being

Glucose is released, requiring insulin from the pancreas. Over a prolonged period, excessive release of glucose may contribute to diabetic conditions.

The body releases cholesterol into the blood for energy. This cholesterol can be deposited as plaque on the walls of arteries. At the same time, the blood clotting mechanism steps up so you won't immediately bleed to death if physically injured. Most of our stresses today do not involve physical injury, and over the long haul, excessive cholesterol deposits and blood clotting increase the possibility for strokes and heart attacks.

> Stress hormones break down body tissue to provide energy for fight and survival, suppress the immune system, and even decrease learning and memory.

The stress hormones adrenaline and cortisol are released, and begin to break down body tissue to provide energy for fight and survival (thus aging us). They suppress the immune system, and even decrease learning and memory[10]. Thus major 21st century diseases and aging itself become offshoots of the stress response.

2. Response Stage Signals

If you take action—fight the attacker, resolve the dilemma—the stress hormones dissipate. Remember, when primitive man confronted a wild animal, he used up those stress hormones constructively, defending himself from the attack. Once the danger was resolved, his body systems returned to normal. Early man's survival challenges were unending and correspondingly, his life expectancy was short and not necessarily sweet. His reaction to stress had to be direct, or he would not live to tell the tale.

However, in our century, we aren't facing tigers. Most stresses today are different, often not allowing for immediate action. Like the underlying insecurity caused by the threat of terrorism, or dealing with an unappreciative boss or a difficult family member over the long-term, where the fight/flight responses are not appropriate. We have little time to deal with the many demands on our system: Negative news on TV, stressful driving, toxic foods, polluted environment, stressful jobs and relationships. While we are trapped into back brain reactive survival patterns, the stress is ongoing, and new ideas and choices, a front brain activity, are impossible. Without stress releasing techniques in our lives, the stress hormones will continue to build until we go into overwhelm.

> Most stresses today do not allow for immediate action. Without stress management in our lives, stress hormones continue to build until we go into overwhelm.

3. Overwhelm Stage Signals

Your body has been pushed to the limit by your lack of action: You have not used up those stress hormones in 'flight or fight'. At this point stress hormones have built up to a dangerous level, and your body must detoxify. Blood leaves the large skeletal muscles and moves to the organs of detoxification and elimination—the lungs, liver, kidneys and skin. You feel lethargic and have to sit down, going from mild into more serious overwhelm, and may eventually even faint. Fainting (often part of the initial, shocked alarm stage) is actually an effective defense mechanism. Fainting is the body's way of getting you out of the picture so you stop generating—and start eliminating—the stress hormones.

> Overwhelm Stage: Blood leaves the large skeletal muscles and moves to the organs of detoxification and elimination—the lungs, liver, kidneys, and skin.

Did you notice: *Feeling weak, unbalanced or faint? Was it hard to hold up your arms for a minute?* Unlocking muscles and weakness are classic signs of neurological confusion and overwhelm.

Did you notice: *Feeling clammy or sweaty?* The skin is an organ of elimination. Stress hormones trigger your sweat glands, particularly the armpits and palms of the hands, causing you to feel a cold sweat.

Instead of cursing our bodies for manifesting symptoms of stress, let us thank them for serving us as well as they do for our survival in the moment. Don't condemn the messenger! We should also be grateful for the 'red alert' that we must do something about the stress we're under.

The picture is coming into even clearer focus. You have taken a close look at the non-serving behaviors that have been exacerbated by current events and the loss of societal security. You have identified and/or experienced the unique mental, emotional and physiological reactions of your system to stress. You have a better understanding of what caused those symptoms. Now, let's start tangibly acting upon this insight. The 'proactive' process of neutralizing the non-serving symptoms and extinguishing the Fire, starts now.

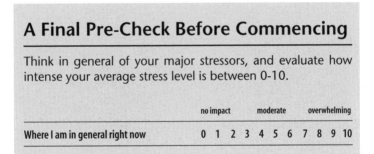

A Final Pre-Check Before Commencing

Think in general of your major stressors, and evaluate how intense your average stress level is between 0-10.

	no impact	moderate	overwhelming
Where I am in general right now	0 1 2 3	4 5 6	7 8 9 10

SECTION 3

FIRE EXTINGUISHERS

Reeducating Your
Brain/Body Response

FIRE EXTINGUISHERS
Reeducating Your
Brain/Body Response

How to Use These Activities

These top activities for stress release have been chosen from the field of Specialized Kinesiology because of their simplicity and usefulness. Each of the activities has been designed to activate a particular energy system of the body. They are presented in a logical sequence. That does not mean you can't go directly to an activity further down the list, if it seems right for you at the moment. Trust your intuition.

The first 10 Fire Extinguishers have been taught as 'The Top 10 Stress Releasers' to schools, corporations and individuals around the world for the past 15 years. For a calm and integrated sense of well-being, activities 1, 2, 3, 4, 6 & 9 should be used regularly. We have grouped them together as the 'Quick Six' on page 183 for later review.

> For a calm and integrated sense of well-being, activities 1, 2, 3, 4, 6 and 9 should be used regularly. We group them together as the 'Quick Six' on page 183 for easy review.

As mentioned in our introduction, the only expert on you is you. There should never be any pain as you do these activities. So take self-responsibility for your own comfort at all times, and be congruent with the advice of your licensed medical practitioner. You are developing new neural connections, improving the message transmission between the brain and body, and subtle movement stimulation activates the circuits as effectively as large movements. You will still notice the difference.

With repetition, these activities further myelinate (put a thick protective coating) on the new brain pathways to make them even more efficient and faster. The stronger the pathways become, the less you need the intervention of the Fire Extinguishers. In other words, the more you use these simple techniques, the less you will need to use them, as you will have established strong new brain patterns that can do the job for you.

Meet Some Energy Switches

First a word about the energy switches in these activities that will make a difference to your brain/body functioning.

Like a light switch completes a circuit allowing free flow of power, these switches open channels of optimal brain/body communication.

Movement: The first and most basic 'energy switch' is simple movement. Body movement stimulates the 'feel good' chemical messengers of our system. Endorphins are the natural opiate manufactured by the body, and production is stimulated by movement, as the famous 'runner's high' confirms. Other brain integration benefits will become apparent later, supporting our use of targeted body movement and natural process to help enhance the manufacture, balance and transportation of chemical messengers (and the flow of subtle balanced energy) in the body.

> We use targeted body movement and natural process to help enhance the manufacture, balance and transportation of chemical messengers (and the flow of subtle balanced energy) in the body.

Touch for Health Energy Switches

Many of the key energy switches for freeing brain/body communication are drawn from the Touch for Health Kinesiology synthesis. All of these techniques, described below, are accessing and working with surface subtle energy systems, which in turn access and impact other interconnected systems, releasing energy blocks on deeper levels.

Neurolymphatic Reflexes[11]: The lymphatic system is the body's recycling system, designed to gather up dead cells, waste from the cells and excess water, and to carry them to the bloodstream. Neurolymphatic reflexes (nerve stimulation points enhancing lymph flow) were discovered and mapped out in the 1930s by osteopath Frank Chapman. He related these reflexes to disturbances in the glandular and organ systems. Later Dr. George Goodheart, a chiropractor, correlated these reflexes to specific muscles. He discovered that stimulating these reflexes could also release energy blocks that are adversely affecting the muscles, improving their strength. Proper diet and exercise are also very important for enhancing lymphatic flow.

> Neurolymphatic reflexes enhance the body's recycling system, which gathers up cellular waste, dead cells and excess water, carrying them to the bloodstream.

The neurolymphatic reflexes are points located mainly on the chest in the rib spaces next to the breastbone, and on the back along the spine, and are stimulated by rubbing with a firm pressure in a circular motion with the fingers. When we ask you to massage a spot, it's a good bet you'll be rubbing a neurolymphatic reflex point!

Neurovascular Holding Points[12]: Dr. Terrence Bennett, DC, discovered these points, also in the 1930s. Located mainly on the head, when held lightly with a slight upward stretch, these neurological switches redirect blood flow to their related muscle, organ or gland. Emotional Stress Release Points on page 87 are a good example.

Meridian Energy And Acupressure Points[13]: Body energy has been charted as flowing in specific pathways we call meridians. There are acupuncture points along these meridians, electromagnetic in character, almost like signaling towers of a transmitting system to specific organs, muscles and functions. Traditional acupuncturists use needles to stimulate or sedate these systems, depending upon how the symptoms of energy blockage have manifested. Don't worry: No needles used here! We can hold, massage or tap acupressure points (as we do in Fear Tapping Points on page 119) to stimulate the release of endorphins, to create analgesia (pain relief), and to release blocked energy.

> Meridians are flowing pathways of body energy. Acupuncture points along them stimulate or sedate specific body organs, muscles and functions.

Muscle Spindle Cell Reflex Technique[14]: The spindle cell is a specialized nerve cell that monitors the muscle's length and the rate of change in its length. This part of the proprioceptive system helps tell us where we are in space. (We will use this mechanism to experiment with the efficiency of our brain/body communication later in the book). The technique is also valuable to relax muscles when they cramp.

> The spindle cell mechanism senses position and tension within a muscle, and helps us know where we are in space.

See if you can identify which energy switches are in full operation as you experience each of the Brain Body Balancers that follow.

How Will You Know if These Activities Help You?

Make a point of Noticing: Do you feel better? How are you performing in your daily activities? Are you more effective? Are things easier? That's how you'll know. Remember our Information Sandwich: Check how you feel before doing each of the Fire Extinguishers and then do the brief insight activity after the experience to notice the difference.

So once again, think of your key stressor identified on page 37. Keep it in mind as you reeducate your responses with the activities that follow. The reeducation process starts now.

ACTIVITY   DRINK WATER

Why: Water is the #1 stress buster and brain integrator. Water provides the hydration necessary to conduct the electrical impulses throughout the body, impulses that carry orders from the brain to the muscles and feedback to the brain. Without proper hydration, you'll feel short-circuited and will trigger a stress response, even without other stressors in your life! What's more, pure water is sensed by the brain while still in your mouth via receptors, and instantly corrects the body stress created by dehydration. In the words of Dr. John Thie, author of *Touch For Health*, "We can't substitute other liquids for water any more than we would want to fill the battery in the car with milk, the steam iron with tomato juice, or wash the walls with coffee."

> We can't substitute other liquids for water any more than we would want to fill the battery in the car with milk, the steam iron with tomato juice, or wash the walls with coffee.

Water is essential for proper lymphatic function, helping to remove waste and toxins from the body. It also allows 1,000-10,000 times more oxygen to bind to the blood, reducing stress on the heart and lungs. An instant brain boost, drinking lots of water heightens energy, improves concentration, mental and physical coordination, and academic skills. It's especially helpful while working with electrical machines (e.g. computers) which can negatively affect our body.

How: If you have no medical limitations, doctors suggest one ten-ounce glass per day for every 30 pounds of body weight, and more if one is physically active or under stress. Therefore the average 150 lb. person needs at least five glasses of water per day (most would say 8 glasses). Caffeine and alcohol, by the way, are diuretics and you will need an extra glass of water for each cup of coffee you drink and two extra glasses for each alcoholic drink.

FIRE EXTINGUISHER 1: DRINK WATER

- *Daily: One 10 oz. glass for every 30 lbs of body weight OR one 250 ml glass for every 10 kg of body weight*

- *Plus: 1 glass for each cup of coffee or caffeinated drink*

- *Plus: 2 glasses for every alcoholic drink*

- *More if you are exercising heavily or under stress*

Variations in Real Life: Drink bottled water instead of pop. Always carry a bottle filled with good quality filtered water wherever you go. Learning experts are now aware of how vital water is for state management and learning. So take that fact to the office for better performance: The old cliche of gathering around the water cooler is not such a bad idea for an office break. Go with the flow of H_2O.

FIRE EXTINGUISHER 1: REVIEW

	uncomfortable							comfortable		
My sense of ease **before** doing this activity	0 1 2 3 4 5 6 7 8 9 10									
My sense of ease **after** doing this activity	0 1 2 3 4 5 6 7 8 9 10									

Any differences I noticed:

_____

PLUG IN FOR BALANCED ENERGY

ACTIVITY 2

FIRE EXTINGUISHER

Why: "Plugging In" helps to normalize the energy flow on key energy meridians, and to minimize the stress response. This simple activity helps you feel more alert, clearer and centered. It can help integrate your left and right brain hemispheres, activate visual centers and strengthen muscles. It's great when your thinking gets fuzzy, or you feel confused.

How: Make a claw with one hand, and point in with your five fingertips in a circle around your navel, with your thumb closer to your head. We have strong nerve end-

> "Plugging in" can help integrate your left and right brain hemispheres, activate visual centers, and strengthen muscles by releasing meridian energy blockages.

ings under our fingernails, and this allows those nerves to be in contact with your acupuncture energy system. Continue to point inward for the next two steps.

FIRE EXTINGUISHER 2: PLUG IN FOR BALANCED ENERGY

photo 1

1. *Make a claw with one hand, and point in with your five fingertips in a circle around your navel, with your thumb closer to your head. Continue to point inward for the next two steps.*

2. *Massage the acupressure points in the hollows just below the collarbone, on either side of the breastbone— between your first and second ribs (photo 1).*

photo 2

3. *Then, massage above and below the lips (photo 2).*

1. For Left/Right Integration: Massage the acupressure points in the hollows just below the collarbone, on either side of the breastbone—between your first and second ribs. These Kidney 27 acupressure points are considered master association points to the entire acupuncture system. Massaging them is believed to affect flow of blood (and oxygen) to the brain.

2. For Up/Down and Front/Back Brain Integration: Massage above and below the lips. You are stimulating the ends of the Central (front) and Governing (back) energy meridians of the body.

This technique was developed by Hap and Elizabeth Barhydt. See their book *Self-Help for Stress & Pain*.

Variations in Real Life:

1. While in a meeting drop one hand to your lap and casually position it over the navel. With other hand massage the points below your collarbone, one side at a time.

2. Lean your elbow on table or desk, and press on points above and below your lips. You may look like Rodin's thinker, but you're really activating key circuits.

Brain Buttons™

3. Brain Buttons™ are part of the PACE process used by Brain Gym® (see page 184). Place the palm of your hand flat over your navel. Massage the K27 points (below collarbone, right and left sides of the breastbone) as described in Step 1. The points massaged are aptly called Brain Buttons by students, as they promote clearer thinking.

FIRE EXTINGUISHER 2: REVIEW

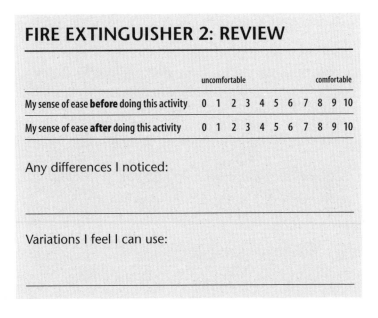

	uncomfortable								comfortable		
My sense of ease **before** doing this activity	0	1	2	3	4	5	6	7	8	9	10
My sense of ease **after** doing this activity	0	1	2	3	4	5	6	7	8	9	10

Any differences I noticed:

Variations I feel I can use:

CROSS PATTERNING　　ACTIVITY **3**

Why: This Cross Patterning technique from Three In One Concepts is simple to learn and activates communication between the two brain hemispheres and the whole body. It works by stimulating the brain to shift between integrated (two-sided) processing, using a cross lateral (two-sided) march, and parallel (one-sided) processing using a unilateral (one-sided) march. Use it whenever you find it hard to "do" and "think" at the same time.

Each brain hemisphere controls the opposite side of the body. So by intentionally moving an opposite arm and leg across the

> By intentionally moving an opposite arm and leg across the midfield, we fire off both brain hemispheres at the same time, creating and myelinating better neural connections between the two.

midfield (vertical center line) of our body, we fire off both left and right brain hemispheres at the same time, creating and myelinating better neural connections between the two.

This cross lateral movement stimulates the whole brain—the vestibular (balance) system, the reticular activating system (the brain's wake-up call), the cerebellum (automatic movement), the basal ganglia (intentional movement), the limbic system (emotional balance), and the frontal lobes (reasoning). Slow cross lateral movement also increases dopamine levels in the brain, enhancing our ability to see patterns and to learn faster. Dopamine is one of the neurotransmitters for which millions of children, diagnosed as ADD or ADHD, take Ritalin to balance. Targeted activity can help restore this balance naturally.

When we then switch to a same side arm and leg movement, we deepen the neural netting that assures our ability to quickly shift with ease and full access, to each individual hemisphere as needed. The intent is never to be 'stuck' in any one pattern of brain communication. Multiple connections and instant flexibility are the key!

How: If you are physically challenged, you may do this technique sitting or lying down, using small arm and leg movements. If totally unable to move, visualizing the activity will also stimulate the appropriate pathways.

1. Start off with a cross march (commonly called cross crawl), slowly and deliberately crossing the right arm over the midline of the body to touch the thigh of the raised left leg. Release that arm

FIRE EXTINGUISHER 3: CROSS PATTERNING

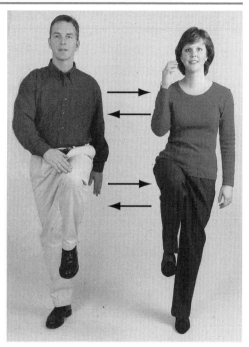

1. *Do a set of cross march, moving right arm to touch the left knee, then the left arm to touch the right knee, very deliberately and slowly.*

2. *Switch to one-sided march (same-sided hand and leg move together, like a puppet on a string) also very deliberately and slowly.*

3. *Alternate sets 6 or 7 times.*

4. *Always finish on the cross march.*

and leg, and deliberately lift the opposite arm and leg, left arm to touch the right thigh. Do 6 or 7 repetitions of this cross march sequence with deliberate, controlled movements and relaxed shoulders. This constitutes one set. Notice if it is automatic and easy, or if it requires deliberate thought and effort.

2. Switch over to a one-sided march. In a controlled manner raise the same side hand and leg together, then lower them. Now raise the other side's arm and leg together, and lower. Imagine being a puppet on a string. Do 6 or 7 repetitions of this alternating sequence, for one set. This fires off one side of the brain at a time. Notice how it feels. Does it require conscious intent, or is it effortless?

3. Now alternate between a full set of cross marching and a full set of one-sided marching, 6 or 7 times or until the shift is smooth. Always end on cross march.

Our goal is to automatically do the cross march without having to think about it, yet to be able to stop and intentionally switch to the one-sided march with ease—a necessary step for the processing of new information.

Many variations, like touching your elbow to your opposite knee, or reaching behind your back to touch your hand to the opposite heel, can be used to keep cross marching fun and fresh.

Doing Cross Patterning slowly and deliberately in the beginning heightens the benefit as it brings in the issues of balance, and acute awareness of your position in space. Later, after the process has become automatic, you can use fast, upbeat music for variety and sheer fun.

Variation of Cross March

Some people find it is stressful to use both sides of the brain and body at the same time. This often mirrors a difficulty in a sharing of information between the left and right brain hemispheres, causing one to be overly dominant. Whether the winner is the logical/scientist or the whole picture/artist hemisphere, remember you're losing up to 70% of the input of the other side—not good for optimum functioning[15].

If you experience difficulty with this activity, it is a sure sign that you stand to benefit greatly from our brain/body activities. A session with a Specialized Kinesiologist for more profound repatterning procedures could also prove extremely beneficial.

Variations in Real Life:

1. Reactivate your brain hemispheres anytime, anywhere, by simply flicking an opposite finger and toe, using minute movements. No one will notice your subtle self-care as you sit at a desk or a table in a board, examination or waiting room—even on the bus. Remember to alternate a set of cross march with a set of one sided march, flicking the same sided finger and toe, and you've done a full cross patterning.

A subtle variation of cross march, flicking opposite finger and toe.

2. While alternating between the cross march and the one-sided march, think of any stressful situation—a presentation, sales call, examination, meeting, etc., then use positive affirmations to further aid stress management. For some sample affirmations, see the Addenda section, pages 208–210.

3. Use this technique while memorizing, to anchor two-dimensional abstract learning into the three-dimensional moving body.

4. Cross March (or Cross Crawl), the first half of cross patterning, has been used for years by educators as a prime brain integrator. Take this easy path to a clear mind. Cross March is available to you every time you take a walk, so take one whenever you can, swinging your arms freely. A treadmill is excellent when safety or weather keeps you indoors. If you have access to one, use it not just when you are doing aerobic exercise, but for a quick brain integration break anytime.

FIRE EXTINGUISHER 3: REVIEW

	uncomfortable									comfortable	
My sense of ease **before** doing this activity	0	1	2	3	4	5	6	7	8	9	10
My sense of ease **after** doing this activity	0	1	2	3	4	5	6	7	8	9	10

Any differences I noticed:

Variations I feel I can use:

ACTIVITY 4 — POLARIZED BREATHING

Why: Deep, rhythmic breathing has long been recommended for stress control and relaxation. Less well known is that our breathing pattern changes from one nostril to the other regularly. This ensures an ionization balance, which in turn affects the balance of calcium and phosphorus in the blood. With stress, the polarization goes off, and body imbalances begin.

Research has shown that breathing through the nose cools the hypothalamus, which monitors brain chemicals that influence mood (*APA Monitor*, Oct. 1990). The breathing cycle is linked to hemispheric dominance in the brain. Right nostril (left hemisphere) dominance correlates to phases of increased activity. Left nostril (right hemisphere) dominance represents rest phases. To change your mood, breathe through your more congested nostril[16].

> Right nostril dominance correlates to phases of increased activity. Left nostril dominance represents rest phases. To change your mood, breathe through your more congested nostril.

It has been clinically demonstrated that this technique can help balance the brain and body for relaxation and more efficient thinking. Polarized Breathing was first used in Applied Kinesiology by Dr. Sheldon Deal[17].

How:

1. Put your tongue on the roof of your mouth.

2. Hold one nostril shut and breathe in, then hold other nostril shut to breathe out. Repeat 3 times.

3. Change sides. Breathe in through nostril previously exhaling, and out through the opposite nostril. Repeat 3 times.

FIRE EXTINGUISHER 4: POLARIZED BREATHING

1. Put your tongue on the roof of your mouth.

2. Hold one nostril shut and breathe in, then hold other nostril shut to breathe out. Repeat 3 times.

3. Change sides. Breathe in through nostril previously exhaling, and out through the opposite nostril. Repeat 3 times.

Variations in Real Life:

Wipe Your Nose: You can pretend to wipe your nose, unobtrusively closing the left nostril, forcing air through your right nostril for more activity in the logical brain, if reasoning or speaking is required. If you feel nervous and more relaxation is required, close off the right nostril, breathing deeply through the left nostril[18].

Deep Breathing: Two thirds of the cells that receive oxygen into the blood stream are located in the bottom third of the lungs. So take deep, steady diaphragmatic breaths whenever and wherever you feel a negative stress reaction. A bonus: Deep breathing also massages your internal organs.

A deep, purposeful yawn will help oxygenate your system and relax tight jaw muscles.

Yawning: A deep, purposeful yawn will help oxygenate your system and relax tight jaw muscles. All vision enhancement programs recommend yawning, as it stimulates tear production, refreshing tired eyes.

FIRE EXTINGUISHER 4: REVIEW

	uncomfortable							comfortable			
My sense of ease **before** doing this activity	0	1	2	3	4	5	6	7	8	9	10
My sense of ease **after** doing this activity	0	1	2	3	4	5	6	7	8	9	10

Any differences I noticed:

_____

Variations I feel I can use:

_____

ACTIVITY 5   COOK'S HOOK-UPS

Why: This activity enables you to bring all the energy meridians into a more balanced state. Use it any time you are upset, sad or confused. You are linking up front/back, up/down and left/right connections into a figure 8. Electrical energy will begin to flow easily along the pathways, and you may sense increased circulation through your extremities. You are using your own body's electrical forces to normalize energy flow as you deal with thoughts or issues that previously would have blown your circuits. Cook's Hook-ups was developed by Wayne Cook and is especially useful for people who exhibit severe electromagnetic imbalances.

> You are using your body's own electrical forces to normalize energy flow as you deal with thoughts or issues that previously would have blown your circuits.

How: Begin by sitting in a comfortable chair with your feet flat on the floor.

Position 1

1. Put one ankle over the other knee.

2. Use the opposite arm to grasp the bent leg's ankle.

3. Bend the other arm, and reach over to grasp the ball of the bent leg's foot.

4. Put your tongue on the roof of your mouth and breathe deeply.

5. Hold this position and think of your stressor for a minute or two, or until you feel calm. If you feel like it, reverse the posture.

When you feel relaxed, move to Position 2, keeping your tongue on the roof of your mouth.

Position 2

1. Uncross your legs and place your feet flat on the floor, tongue remaining on the roof of your mouth.

2. Put the tips of your fingers together gently and breathe deeply. As well as being highly energized, the ends of our fingertips have alternating polarities on opposing hands (thumbs are neutral). When you hold your fingertips together it completes a circuit, and energy flows from the positive to the negative polarity. After a few minutes your fingertips may get rosy and you may feel a throb from moving energy. This is a wonderful posture if you experience cold extremities!

3. Once you have assumed this position, think of your stressor once again, for a minute or two or until you sigh, yawn, or feel even more relaxed.

FIRE EXTINGUISHER 5: COOK'S HOOK-UPS

Position 1

*Put one ankle over the other knee. Use the
opposite arm to grasp the bent leg's ankle. Bend
the other arm, and reach over to grasp the ball
of the bent leg's foot. Put your tongue on the
roof of your mouth and breathe deeply. If you
feel like it, reverse the posture. When you feel
relaxed, move to Position 2.*

Position 2

*Uncross your legs. Keep your tongue on the
roof of your mouth. Put your fingertips together
gently and breathe deeply. Hold each position
for a minute or two or until you feel calm.*

Variation for standing up or lying down—great when you're having trouble getting to sleep

Cross your left wrist over your right wrist and your left ankle over your right ankle (or vice versa). Turn the palms of your hands to face each other and interlace your fingers. Turn your hands in toward

your body and up. Put the tip of your tongue on the roof of your mouth behind your teeth. Breathe deeply, and when you feel relaxed, move to Position 2 as described previously. This variation, called Hook-ups, was developed by Dr. Paul and Gail Dennison for Brain Gym®. It is used with great effect as part of the PACE™ process on p. 184.

Variation for standing up or lying down—great when you're having trouble getting to sleep

Variation in Real Life:

Seated anywhere, even in the boardroom: loosely cross your legs or your ankles, and cross your arms to casually rest your hands on your thighs. You are making subtle left/right up/down cross over connections. No one knows you're holding your tongue to the roof of your mouth when not speaking. You can then replicate position 2 by sitting with your feet flat on the floor, hands in your lap with fingertips touching.

Real life variations you can do almost anywhere– even in a meeting

FIRE EXTINGUISHER 5: REVIEW

	uncomfortable		comfortable
My sense of ease **before** doing this activity	0 1 2 3 4 5 6	7 8 9 10	
My sense of ease **after** doing this activity	0 1 2 3 4 5 6	7 8 9 10	

Any differences I noticed:

_____

Variations I feel I can use:

_____

HOLD YOUR EMOTIONAL STRESS RELEASE POINTS

ACTIVITY

Whenever you feel under pressure, hurt or shocked, take the emotional edge off by holding your Emotional Stress Release Points, also called Positive Points™ in Brain Gym®. Emotional Stress Release was first presented in Touch For Health in the early 1970s, and involves holding the neurovascular holding points that balance both the Central (mental) and Stomach (digestive) energy meridians. Remember, neurovascular holding points redirect blood flow to their related organ.

Why: The light holding of your hands to your forehead help pull the blood supply and therefore the fuel for the brain (oxygen and glucose) to the frontal planning lobes. This stops the classic stress response, (which diverts blood flow straight to the back brain survival centers) right in its tracks. With Emotional Stress Release you can perceive new ideas, and make creative choices even when you're under stress.

> Scientific evidence supports the idea that what we imagine is as real to our brain as what we have actually experienced.

We seem to do this instinctively—the "Oh No!" response, when we put a hand automatically to our forehead when shocked. We just have to learn to do it on purpose, and hold our hand or hands there, keeping front-brained while we think through our stressor.

Scientific evidence supports the idea that what we imagine is as real to our brain as what we have actually experienced: PET scans, CAT scans, MRIs, etc., show virtually the same brain activity for both real and imagined activity. Therefore, we can break the hold of stressful memory or fear by imagining as many changes as possible to the memory lock, thus creating and reinforcing new brain connections.

FIRE EXTINGUISHER 6: HOLD YOUR EMOTIONAL STRESS RELEASE POINTS

1. *Put your fingertips gently on your forehead, above your eyebrows.*

2. *Tug up slightly on the skin, while you think through your problem, pre-rehearse a successful outcome, or talk it out.*

Visualize a positive outcome with lots of sensory detail to create the new 'reality' you deserve. Always remember to notice the improvements in how you feel physically and mentally after the process, to help anchor in your brain/body's new improved functioning.

How:

1. Put your fingertips gently on your forehead, above your eyebrows.

2. Tug up slightly on the skin, while you think through your problem, pre-rehearse a successful outcome, or talk it out.

Stress Releasing the Future

Hold your Emotional Stress Release Points while you mentally rehearse an upcoming challenge—a formerly fearful situation, a presentation, a test, an interview, a race—any situation where you want to be calm and focused. From beginning to end, anticipate everything that could happen, good or bad, every step of the way. See yourself handling all possibilities with coolness and grace. See your successful completion with as much sensory detail as possible. Awareness of colors, sounds, smells, tastes and body sensations while holding your Emotional Stress Release Points, activates more areas of the brain which could be tied into a stress circuit lock.

Combining Mental Rehearsal with Emotional Stress Release creates a rocket trajectory to excellence. Athletes, sports coaches, educators and psychologists have already proved Mental Rehearsal effective. Thinking fires off the same circuits as doing. Adding Emotional Stress Release to Mental Rehearsal assures we are programming our imagined action in as a whole-brained, integrated activity with access to the frontal cortex for new solutions. Defuse the bad memories or possibilities, so you can keep front-brained when you think of the situation, and infuse the good outcomes, to lay down positive neural 'memory' traces throughout the brain.

> Thinking fires off the same circuits as doing. Combining Mental Rehearsal with Emotional Stress Release creates a rocket trajectory to excellence.

Stress Releasing the Past

The powerful techniques that follow are drawn from many counseling modalities. I was introduced to their effectiveness in my training with Three In One Concepts.

A) *Change the outcome*

This technique can be used to defuse the 'stuck circuit lock' triggered by any stressful memory or fear. All you need do is to hold your Emotional Stress Release Points while you remember the incident, until you notice yourself feeling more relaxed. Next, change the outcome by imagining in detail the scenario you would have preferred, making as many positive changes as possible to the old stressful memory. You break the cycle of the old memory by adding in new information and an overlay of a more positive ending. It didn't happen that way, you say? What does it matter, if the process creates new brain patterns, and frees you from recycling non-serving emotional responses.

> Change the outcome by imagining in detail the scenario you would have preferred. You break the cycle of the old memory by adding in new information and an overlay of a more positive ending.

B) Creating a safety zone

In all cases it is good to create an escape hatch in case you find a personal process getting too intense for comfort. The Anchoring activity on page 107 is a great way to create a source of positive energy before attempting to deal with a serious issue. Another wonderful technique adapted from Neuro Linguistic Programming is to create an imaginary circle around yourself that serves as a boundary to contain your negative situation. If you feel any sense of overwhelm as you think of your issue, just get up and physically step out of the circle, away from the problem and back into the present time and room. Breathe deeply. Use your Fire Extinguishers to regain your composure before continuing. Choose one of the more in-depth techniques below, before reentering that circle to resume your process.

> Create an imaginary circle around yourself that serves as a boundary to contain your negative situation. If you feel any sense of overwhelm as you think of your issue, physically step out of the circle.

Also note: It's a good idea to sit in a different part of the room than where you normally sit and work. Memory is strongly triggered by location. Teachers are trained to stand in a different place in the room while disciplining students, so the teaching space is not contaminated with negative association. Similarly, that psychological circle you've created might temporarily take on a subconscious negativity, and you may want to be able to move away from it when you're done.

C) *Viewing and editing a video*

Imagine yourself as viewing a video of the memory or event. You have a remote control in your hand, and the ability to start or stop at any time, fast forward or edit out any unwanted influences. You are the writer, producer and director. Create a positive outcome. Throw a pie in the face of the villain. This technique is particularly effective because it gives you the security of being an observer and in control, rather than helplessly reliving the experience.

D) *Reframing the picture*

If you find it impossible to imagine a more positive scenario, snap a mental picture of the trigger situation. Notice as much detail as possible in that picture. Now imagine placing that static picture in a frame, and describe the frame to yourself. Metal or wood? What color? Simple or carved? Large or small? Once you are clear in your mind what that frame looks like, change it in your mind's eye. Picture it in a different material, color, design and size. This should be easy, as you do

> Snap a mental picture of the trigger situation. Imagine placing that static picture in a frame, and imagine the frame to yourself in great detail. Then, consciously change the details of the frame.

not have an emotional investment in the frame. Then take another look at the picture in the frame. Can you change the color of the background? Put different clothing on the people in the picture, or change their position? Now proceed to change other details in color and content. Then proceed to viewing and editing the whole memory as if it were a video as described above, changing the frightening elements into something soothing.

E) Dividing the pie

When dealing with a truly overwhelming trauma, it is good to divide the memories down into chunks that you can handle without overwhelm. For instance, rather than stress releasing a particular picture, or running the whole memory as a movie, divide it down into its components—what you heard, what you felt, what you saw, what you smelled—one little sensory part of the overall memory at a time. When that image has lost its ability to trigger physical discomfort, move on to another image frozen in your memory. Then move on to the sounds you heard, followed by the smells you smelled, the physical impact you experienced, etc. Stress release each piece until you can think of it without triggering the stress

> Divide an overwhelming memory down into its components—what you heard, what you felt, what you saw, what you smelled—one little sensory part of the overall memory at a time.

response. At this point you can change little parts of the memory. Changing the image in a positive way in your mind gives you some sense of control. Only then put all the memories back together and view them as a movie or video in your mind, running it forward, then backward, then changing it to create a more acceptable scenario.

F) Touch the feeling

When you are experiencing physiological signals of stress and have no memory of the stressful trigger, trust your Noticing of where the stress response is located in your body, and touch where you feel it most intensely. Follow through with basic stress release, holding your forehead with your other hand, until the feeling has been neutralized, and physiological indicators have eased.

Touch the feeling

G) *Postural Stress Release*

When stress releasing a physical trauma or accident, it is very effective to assume the posture or body position you were thrown into after the impact. The cellular memory in the body may be holding pain signals, even though the physiology has since healed. If you cannot remember the actual positions involved, just make it up. Your conscious mind may not remember, but you can trust your body to lead you to an appropriate posture.

Postural Stress Release

Other variations:

1. A powerful variation of ESR, from Three in One
   Concepts, is called Frontal/Occipital Holding.
   Lightly hold your forehead with one hand and
   hold your other hand over your visual cortex at
   the back turn of the skull. This draws energy to
   the primary visual cortex, the area of the brain
   that must "see" clearly what really happened or
   visualize the best future action if you are to make
   successful choices and plans (a front brain activity) in the light of what you already know.

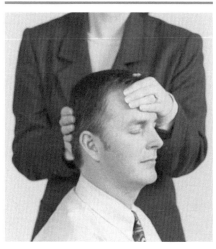

Frontal/Occipital Holding

2. For powerful emotional stress management you can also have someone hold your ESR points (or Frontal/Occipital Holding), while you do Cook's Hook-ups (page 80), or Hook-ups (page 84). The cross linking of limbs achieved by Cook's Hook-ups balances all the meridian energy in the body, while your partner's holding of your Emotional Stress Release Points makes sure energy stays in the front cerebral cortex for better thinking and creative problem solving. Thus both body and brain are assured a balanced energy flow while you process your issue.

Variations in Real Life:

Last thing before you go to bed: Defuse any stresses from your day, and start to jot down your 'to do' list for the next day. You will then settle into more restful sleep.

First thing when you get up: Plan your day using Emotional Stress Release to keep yourself front-brained and thinking clearly.

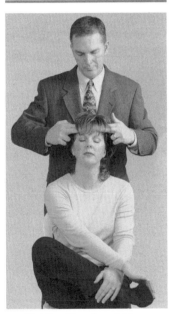

Holding Emotional Stress Release (ESR) points while doing Cook's Hook-ups

Pain relief: For minor bumps and ouches, hold pain spot with one hand, and forehead with the other. Great for soothing children.

Writing: If you are writing under pressure due to a test or deadline, rest your forehead on one hand while you write with your other hand.

FIRE EXTINGUISHER 6: REVIEW

	uncomfortable								comfortable	
My sense of ease **before** doing this activity	0 1 2 3 4 5 6 7 8 9 10									
My sense of ease **after** doing this activity	0 1 2 3 4 5 6 7 8 9 10									

Any differences I noticed:

_____

Variations I feel I can use:

_____

_____

_____

ACTIVITY EYE ROTATIONS

Why: Coupling the holding of your ESR points with eye rotations takes Emotional Stress Release a step deeper. A growing number of psychological methodologies use eye movement as their major tool for releasing old patterns.

A quick example: One dramatic example of the power of defusing eye directions occurred in a class a number of years ago, when a 55 year old woman volunteered for a segment on vision improvement. On asking her to look down, I noticed she became unsteady on her feet. When I asked her to look down to the left, her eyes wouldn't move, and she turned to the left with her whole body instead.

I asked her to sit down and to assume the Cook's Hook-ups posture. I held her head with Frontal/Occipital holding. I then asked her to look down to the left. She complied, then trembled and burst into tears. After several minutes, she shared that as a young woman of 22 she had gone swimming, stumbling on something soft in the knee-deep water as she waded in. She looked down in the water to the left, and saw a drowned body below the surface. Over the intervening years, she had repressed that memory, but her body had not forgotten the trauma of looking down to the left.

The simple stress release procedure we did, plus a few eye activating activities outlined in my book *Making the Brain Body Connection*, manifested weeks later in improved vision (she had to get weaker glasses), and the elimination of her fear of heights. Although this was an unexpected side benefit to the stress defusion, it makes sense that if a person is blocked from looking down, they would fear heights. It can be that simple—and unplanned—to achieve remarkable results from these techniques.

Back to Why: Bits of memory (color, smell, sound, taste, etc.) are embedded throughout the brain. Our eye direction shifts each time we access a different part of the brain. Neuro Linguistic Programming (NLP) delves into specific eye directions needed to access particular memories or functions. A short cut was developed by Dr. Wayne Topping, who determined that all we need do is a full eye rotation, which activates all areas of the brain at once. Take care to extend your eye muscles in all directions.

> Bits of memory (color, smell, sound, taste, etc.) are embedded throughout the brain. Our eye direction shifts each time we access a different part of the brain.

How:

Step 1: Add Eye Rotation to Emotional Stress Release

Slowly and carefully rotate your eyes clockwise and counter-clockwise at least once. Overlap when changing directions. Really extend your eye muscles. Repeat until the eyes rotate smoothly. If you trigger an emotion, feel an eye jerk, pain or avoidance in any one direction, continue looking in that direction while holding your forehead until the stress reaction eases. Don't forget to track left and right as well as up and down to also release those directional locks.

This technique is so simple, you can do it during a TV commercial. Pay particular attention to any direction where the eye doesn't move as freely, or you feel strain.

FIRE EXTINGUISHER 7: EYE ROTATION

Rotate your eyes 360° <u>clockwise</u> and then <u>counter-clockwise</u> while holding forehead.

Make sure you overlap your rotation when changing directions.

Really extend your eye muscles.

Hold that position until the tension eases. You can be stress releasing a particular incident or feeling, or simply clearing your eye modes of subconscious locked-in stress. A wonderful benefit of all these techniques is that we don't

> We have no way of knowing what stuck stress circuits we have locked into each of these eye directions, and it pays to disengage those associations.

have to smell our garbage before we throw it out. We have no way of knowing what stuck stress circuits we have locked into each of these eye directions, and it pays to disengage those associations.

Step 2: Add Affirmations

Program in a quick dose of positive emotion whenever the need arises. Say "I feel *(insert the appropriate emotion or state of being statement)*" while holding your forehead and rotating your eyes. This puts the affirmation directly into the subconscious, and efficiently accesses the whole brain for deep stress release. For example, after narrowly avoiding a car crash, heart pounding, I pulled over to the side of the road and did eye rotations on "I feel calm" and "I feel safe." I was suffused with those feelings, and within two minutes, my stress reaction dissipated and I was able to proceed on my way.

A neutralizing affirmation used in a number of methodologies to correct self-sabotage is:

> "Even though I have this fear of *(insert fear here)*, I deeply and completely love and accept myself."

The affirmation can be generalized for all emotional reversals as follows:

> "Even though I have this *(negative feeling or circumstance)*, I deeply and completely love and accept myself."[19]

Experiment with these statements, in conjunction with your eye rotations.

Until the self-sabotage is released, other improvements you achieve will not hold permanently.

Variations in Real Life: When feeling the onset of overwhelm or a panic attack, find as private a spot as you can. While holding Emotional Stress Release Points and doing eye rotations, use the following affirmations, or others of your choosing:

Affirmations to ease fear and anxiety:
1. I feel safe and secure.
2. I feel calm.
3. I feel strength.
4. I feel self-control.
5. I feel courage.
6. I move through my world with ease and joy.

If you are in a public place or a meeting where you are unable to do eye rotations, hold your Stress Release Points or do another of our unobtrusive activities, and add eye rotations when you are in private, by slipping into the washroom, or the back room at the supermarket.

In a meeting, hold a hand to your forehead, and run your eyes over the lower half of the eye circuit, presumably looking at your notes.

See pages 208–210 in the Addenda for additional affirmations with which to work on your other life issues.

FIRE EXTINGUISHER 7: REVIEW

	uncomfortable								comfortable		
My sense of ease **before** doing this activity	0	1	2	3	4	5	6	7	8	9	10
My sense of ease **after** doing this activity	0	1	2	3	4	5	6	7	8	9	10

Any differences I noticed:

_____

Variations I feel I can use:

_____

I will use the following affirmations:

_____

_____

ANCHORING YOURSELF IN CALM WATERS

Why: Originally derived from Neuro Linguistic Programming (NLP), Anchoring takes advantage of the fact that we lock emotion into the body's cellular memory when experiencing both real and imagined situations. By locking into our body circuits a positive safe place or happy experience, we can quickly infuse any deteriorating situation with a boost of good positive energy, thus breaking the reactive circuit lock triggered by the stressful situation.

> Anchoring takes advantage of the fact that we lock emotion into the body's cellular memory when experiencing both real and imagined situations.

How:

1. Decide on an inconspicuous trigger point that you can access and press in public without calling attention to yourself. Good choices are the top of your thigh or the palm of your hand.

2. Think of your favorite place or happiest time. Vividly recreate it in your mind. See it. Smell it. Hear it. Touch it. Taste it.

3. Firmly push on your anchor point (or points if bilateral) to lock your positive feelings into a physical circuit.

4. When you are under stress and starting to "lose it," press on your anchor point(s) to be flooded with positive energy to counteract your stress, and to avert the negative reactive circuit lock.

Variations in Real Life: Prepare yourself before heading into a potentially stressful situation: In today's world, that might mean before you even get out of bed in the morning! This technique is also an ideal one to use for job interviews and definitely for calm parenting.

FIRE EXTINGUISHER 8: ANCHORING YOURSELF IN CALM WATERS

Think of a positive situation. Press it into cellular memory for easy access when you most need it.

FIRE EXTINGUISHER 8: REVIEW

	uncomfortable							comfortable		
My sense of ease **before** doing this activity	0 1 2 3 4 5 6 7 8 9 10
My sense of ease **after** doing this activity	0 1 2 3 4 5 6 7 8 9 10

Any differences I noticed:

ACTIVITY BE SENSE-ABLE

Why: Our brain hemispheres may be integrated, but are our senses plugged in and switched on? As we have explored, whenever emotion locks into our life experience, the shock to our auditory system and the eye direction we were looking in locks into the body's cellular memory, too. We may forget the trauma, but our bodies and our senses are hindered from optimal processing henceforth. Often, looking in a particular direction or hearing sounds in certain situations, will be stressful. Now we can easily and permanently release the hold these dysfunctional circuits have on us, and refresh our senses from fatigue.

> Whenever emotion locks into our life experience, the shock to our auditory system and the eye direction we were looking in locks into the body's cellular memory, too.

Eye Points

How: For a quick visual 'pick-me-up', massage your 'eye points' at the back of your head, in the hollows above the bony ridge of the lowest turn of your skull (the occipital protuberance). Pressure here stimulates your primary visual cortex, which lies directly below.

Look in all directions as you rub these hollows on the left and right. Also focus on something close and then on something distant, to activate near/far accommodation.

This eye circuit energizer is from Three In One Concepts. Once again remember; if a specific eye direction is uncomfortable, hold your Emotional Stress Release Points until the tension releases.

FIRE EXTINGUISHER 9: EYE POINTS

Massage the hollows above the bony ridge of the lowest turn of your skull (the occipital protuberance).

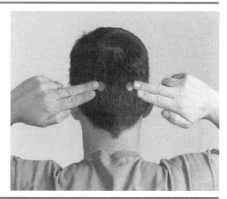

FIRE EXTINGUISHER 9: REVIEW

	uncomfortable									comfortable	
My sense of ease **before** doing this activity	0	1	2	3	4	5	6	7	8	9	10
My sense of ease **after** doing this activity	0	1	2	3	4	5	6	7	8	9	10

Any differences I noticed:

Wake Up Your Ears

Why: Have you ever suddenly realized in the middle of a conversation that you haven't heard a word for several minutes? Whenever you feel your attention wandering, you can refocus your attention by simply massaging your ears.

When you rub your ears you are actually massaging many different acupressure points which stimulate your whole system for a quick pick-me-up. Massage your ears before you have to speak, write, or receive instructions—even when you are silent, because you are always listening to your inner voice. Called The Thinking Cap™ in Brain Gym®, this activity is used by all the major kinesiologies.

How: Gently unroll your ear edges a few times, from top to bottom. Give your ears a light tug to the side. Note how it makes sounds seem brighter and clearer. You will also notice your attention sharpens and you can both hear and think better.

Dr. John Thie, founder of Touch For Health, points out that this auricular exercise can also improve range of motion. Turn your head first to one side, and then the other, as far as you can. Then massage your ears, as you gently turn your head again, looking for—and releasing—any stiffness. After you are done, turn your head again, and notice if you are now rotating further.

> When you rub your ears you are actually massaging many different acupressure points which stimulate your whole system for a quick pick-me-up.

FIRE EXTINGUISHER 9: WAKE UP YOUR EARS

Give your ears a gentle massage, unrolling the edges as well. Turn your head to release neck stress.

Variation in Real Life: When you lose focus and concentration in a meeting or conversation, reach up and discreetly massage one ear at a time. Alternate with rubbing your eye points, one at a time. While we're talking about activating points, don't forget your Kidney 27 acupressure points (on page 66) for electromagnetic balance and visual stimulation as well. If your subtle massage is noticed at all, observers might think you are itchy. They do not know you are managing your state and senses with powerful energizers.

FIRE EXTINGUISHER 9: REVIEW

	uncomfortable									comfortable	
My sense of ease **before** doing this activity	0	1	2	3	4	5	6	7	8	9	10
My sense of ease **after** doing this activity	0	1	2	3	4	5	6	7	8	9	10

Any differences I noticed:

RUB OUT TENSION AND HEADACHES

ACTIVITY

Why: Tension headaches are often caused by emotional stress weakening the front neck muscles, which in turn causes back neck muscles to over-contract. To restore balanced energy to these muscles, get friendly with these neurolymphatic massage points from Touch For Health described in photos 1 and 2 below.

How: If these points are sore, rub them gently, increasing the pressure until the tenderness abates.

Neurolymphatic massage points from Touch For Health

1. The back points are located just where the neck meets the skull on either side of the top vertebra.

2. The front points are under the clavicle (collarbone), half way between the breastbone and the tip of the shoulder.

FIRE EXTINGUISHER 10: RUB OUT TENSION AND HEADACHES

Neurolymphatic Massage Points

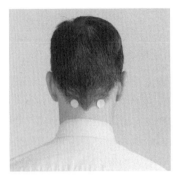

1. *Back points: Where the neck meets the skull.*

2. *Front points: Under the collarbone, halfway to the shoulder just in a natural hollow.*

Acupressure Points

3. *Hand points: On the fleshy web between thumb and index finger.*

4. *Leg points: Standing, where the middle finger of the hand finds a tender spot on the side of thigh.*

Acupressure points

Also useful for eliminating headaches are the following two acupressure points. The hand points (Large Intestine 4), are particularly good for headaches and toothaches. The leg points (Gall Bladder 31), are a key point for toxic conditions and their resulting headaches.

3. The hand points are on the fleshy web between thumb and index finger. (These points are also the key location to attach biodots for a visual feedback of your stress level.)

4. The leg points are known to relieve headaches due to toxicity. To find these important acupressure points on the gall bladder meridian, stand up and let your arms fall to the side of your thighs. With the middle finger of each hand, probe for a sensitive point as low as you can reach on the side of the leg without bending. If you do not find a tender spot (more often the case with men than women) be glad, and stimulate the points anyway. Massage for 7 seconds, and release for 7 seconds, then repeat.

Variations in Real Life: Stimulate those points, one side at a time, as often and as subtly as you can. If you suffer headaches frequently, don't wait until you notice a headache building. Make activating these points part of your daily regime. Remember to get up frequently from your desk or computer, and shift your position to get blood flowing again. Get additional relief from neck and back stress with frequent stretching.

FIRE EXTINGUISHER 10: REVIEW

	uncomfortable							comfortable		
My sense of ease **before** doing this activity	0 1 2 3 4 5 6 7 8 9 10
My sense of ease **after** doing this activity	0 1 2 3 4 5 6 7 8 9 10

Any differences I noticed:

Variations I feel I can use:

FEAR TAPPING POINTS

Why: Activating the ends of the energy meridians for pain relief is a standard technique from acupressure and Touch for Health. It has been found that the stomach meridian is vitally linked to emotional stress. Remember that diversion of energy from digestion, and digestive upset, is one of the first byproducts of the stress response. Thus tapping the ends of the Stomach meridian when fear strikes, stimulates and unblocks the meridian energy system.

> Diversion of energy from digestion is one of the first byproducts of the stress response. Tapping the ends of the Stomach meridian when fear strikes, stimulates and unblocks the meridian energy system.

How: The beginning points of the Stomach meridian are on the cheekbones just under the eyes, and the ends are at the lateral corner of the second toe. This premise has been formalized as the basis for very effective emotional work by Dr. Roger Callahan (*The Five Minute Phobia Cure*), and Gary Craig (*Emotional Freedom Techniques*)[20]. I find an effective simplification of their more in-depth work is to simply tap the facial Fear Tapping points under the eyes. Focus on your fear or situation while firmly tapping with at least two fingers on these bilateral points until the fear symptoms abate.

Variations in Real Life: Tap under both eyes with one hand, using thumb on one side, and index and middle finger together on the other for a neutral polarity. Combine the tapping with affirmations (see page 208).

FIRE EXTINGUISHER 11: FEAR TAPPING POINTS

Tap the beginning points of the stomach meridian on the cheekbones just under the eyes.

FIRE EXTINGUISHER 11: REVIEW

	uncomfortable								comfortable		
My sense of ease **before** doing this activity	0	1	2	3	4	5	6	7	8	9	10
My sense of ease **after** doing this activity	0	1	2	3	4	5	6	7	8	9	10

Any differences I noticed:

Activities That Release the Tendon Guard Reflex

Why: Part of the classic stress response is the tensing of the muscles on the back of our body, from the Achilles tendon in the ankle to the top of the spine and head. This 'fight, flight or freeze' mechanism can cause loss of flexibility and chronic pain. It also locks you into the back survival centers of the brain, the old tapes of the cerebellum determining how you reacted before, cutting off new, more effective solutions.

Freeing the tendon guard reflex immediately relieves a key physiological response of the high alert first stage of stress. It impacts ADD, Hyperactivity, and anxiety.

Freeing the tendon guard reflex immediately relieves a key physiological response of the high alert first stage of stress. I have found this concept vital in dealing with Attention Deficit Disorder and Hyperactivity, as well as relieving anxiety. In the Addenda a brief description is given of how the brain works, and explains further the synergy between releasing the stuck circuit lock of a physical response, and the cascade of improvement that ensues into your emotional and behavioral life[21]. The bottom line: If you don't satisfy the needs of your back brain, energy is not free to move upward for higher brain consideration and function, and you cannot be calm, controlled and at your best.

Spinal flexibility as a metaphor represents one's ability to adapt, to bend rather than break. A flexible spine also encourages the flow of cerebrospinal fluid as these next activities will illustrate. The object is to keep the spine supple, flexible and relaxed, releasing any fixation of the vertebrae.

Variations in Real Life: For all the activities described below, the everyday variation is the same—move, and stretch, stretch, stretch. Unhealthy tension can be released by activities to lengthen our leg, shoulder, spine, abdomen and back muscles. Therefore stretch regularly. Get up at regular intervals, particularly when working at a computer, and stretch your back and neck. When you feel strain or pain, don't wait until after work to take care of it

> Unhealthy tension can be released by activities to lengthen our leg, shoulder, spine, abdomen and back muscles.

at the gym: You can do a calf pump, a hamstring, back or other stretch right in your office, in the moment you first notice the stress response building. The activities below will specifically target and release different aspects of this reflex.

ACTIVITY 12   LEG MUSCLE RELEASE

Why: This activity from Three in One Concepts reeducates the tendon guard response, relaxes the brain stem, and extends your range of motion.

How:

1. Raise your knee as high as you can with your leg bent, bringing your knee toward your chest. Notice the range of motion allowed by your hamstring (the back of your thigh) muscle.

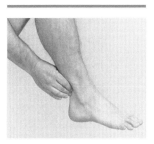

Vigorously pluck the Achilles tendon behind your ankle, between the foot and calf muscle.

2. Vigorously pluck the Achilles tendon behind your ankle, between the foot and calf muscle. For further muscle relaxation, the calf muscle itself can be pinched inward in the vertical direction of the muscle fibers. By doing this, you are activating spindle cell proprioceptors, which send a message to your brain to relax these muscles.

3. Next, pluck the hamstring muscle where you can feel two insertions behind the knee, just a few inches up toward the buttock.

4. Lift your knee again and notice if your leg raises higher comfortably. Repeat the plucking/strumming on the muscle until you are aware of increased flexibility. Follow the same steps with your other leg.

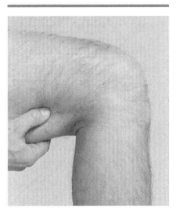

Pluck the hamstring muscle where you can feel two insertions behind the knee, just a few inches up toward the buttock.

FIRE EXTINGUISHER 12: REVIEW

	uncomfortable									comfortable	
My sense of ease **before** doing this activity	0	1	2	3	4	5	6	7	8	9	10
My sense of ease **after** doing this activity	0	1	2	3	4	5	6	7	8	9	10

Any differences I noticed:

ACTIVITY PRIME YOUR SACRAL SPINAL PUMP

Why: Gently rocking back and forth on your buttocks can do great things for your brain. You release the sacrum, which is considered the pump for the cerebrospinal fluid that moves up your central nervous system and through your brain. This fluid transports nutrients, hormones, and neurotransmitters. It also removes toxins from the central nervous system, and cools the brain. Rocking gently on your buttocks helps you loosen up any fixation of the vertebrae after sitting all day, and is good for general body co-ordination.

How: Be self-responsible: If you have a back condition, adapt this activity to simply wiggling on a chair.

1. Sit on the floor on a padded surface. Place your hands behind your hips with fingertips pointing forward.

2. Gently lift your feet off the floor and rock back and forth on alternate buttocks, taking care to protect your tailbone. Rock yourself back and forth as well as in circles until you feel less tense.

FIRE EXTINGUISHER 13: PRIME YOUR SACRAL SPINAL PUMP

1. *Sit on the floor on a padded surface. Place your hands behind your hips with fingertips pointing forward.*

2. *Gently lift your feet off the floor and rock back and forth on alternate buttocks, taking care to protect your tailbone.*

When you feel you have to wiggle in your chair, don't stifle it: Make a point of shifting your weight regularly as you sit throughout the day. This activity is found both in Brain Gym® (called the Rocker™) and Hyperton-X.

FIRE EXTINGUISHER 13: REVIEW

	uncomfortable								comfortable	
My sense of ease **before** doing this activity	0 1 2 3 4 5 6 7 8 9 10
My sense of ease **after** doing this activity	0 1 2 3 4 5 6 7 8 9 10

Any differences I noticed:

FIRE EXTINGUISHER

ACTIVITY 14

THE ENERGIZER™

Why: This activity releases the spine, abdomen and back muscles and can be done easily and safely at your desk. It keeps the spine supple, flexible and relaxed, releasing any fixation of the vertebrae.

1. Put your hands flat on your desk and rest your forehead between your hands.

2. As you breathe in, scoop your neck forward lifting your head up gently.

How:

1. Put your hands flat on your desk and rest your forehead between your hands, curving your spine. Breathe out all your tension.

2. As you breathe in, scoop your neck forward (imagine pushing a ball with your nose), lifting your head up gently, forehead first, followed by your neck and upper body. Your lower body and shoulders remain relaxed. Lengthen the back, vertebra by vertebra.

3. Exhale as you reverse the process. Bend the spine forward, tucking your chin down into your chest to lengthen the back of your neck, and with a fluid motion scoop your head forward once again, repeating the process several times.

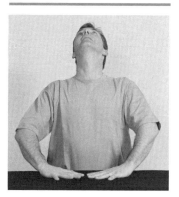

2. (cont'd) Your lower body and shoulders remain relaxed. Lengthen the back, vertebra by vertebra.

The Energizer was developed for the Brain Gym® series of movements for whole brain learning.

FIRE EXTINGUISHER 14: REVIEW

	uncomfortable							comfortable		
My sense of ease **before** doing this activity	0 1 2 3 4 5 6 7 8 9 10
My sense of ease **after** doing this activity	0 1 2 3 4 5 6 7 8 9 10

Any differences I noticed:

ACTIVITY

NECK AND SHOULDER RELEASE

Why: The neck and shoulders are primary targets for stress, and also have key proprioception for vision and hearing, as they turn the head toward sensory stimulation. Tension in the neck can impact listening, comprehension, thinking, memory, speaking and functioning.

How:

1. Let your left ear gently fall toward your left shoulder, only as far as it goes without stress. Your arms rest naturally at your sides.

FIRE EXTINGUISHER 15: NECK AND SHOULDER RELEASE

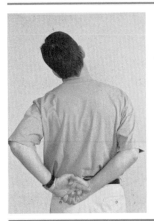

1. Drop your left ear gently toward your shoulder.

2. Gently put your right arm behind your back to enhance your right neck muscle release.

2. Put your right arm behind your back at waist level to enhance the extension you feel in your right neck muscles. Breathe deeply while you hold the position for at least 30 seconds. Repeat on the other side.

3. Gently drop your head to your chest. Slowly rotate your head in a small semi-circle from one shoulder to the other. Hold your extension for a few seconds at any spot that is particularly stressed or tight. The neck is very vulnerable; never roll your neck completely around in a circle, or make jerking movements. Always move slowly and gently.

4. Gently rotate your shoulders where the arm bone inserts with small movements, first in circling forward three or four rotations, then in backward circles.

FIRE EXTINGUISHER 15: REVIEW

	uncomfortable								comfortable		
My sense of ease **before** doing this activity	0	1	2	3	4	5	6	7	8	9	10
My sense of ease **after** doing this activity	0	1	2	3	4	5	6	7	8	9	10

Any differences I noticed:

We have now presented you with 15 of the top Stress Releasers, and over time you will build up a repertoire of favorites. Remember that each activity has been targeted to impact a particular area of imbalance. When you are tired and unfocused, you will need to be energized. When you are on edge and frazzled, you will need to be calmed. Some techniques will prove more effective for you than others in different situations. You may do several activities before you hit the ones that give you the desired result.

The reason we encourage you to automatically turn to the 'Quick Six' (page 183) or the Brain Gym® PACE™ process (page 184), is because they offer you the proper combination of balanced activities when you haven't the time to choose.

Remember, these techniques are designed to restore you to a balanced energy state in the moment. You may re-trigger your response to a stressful issue, and need to repeat the balancing activities a few times. For permanent and long-term handling of deeply etched patterns, repetition and/or a more involved process may be necessary. Extraordinary long-term results are experienced by most, so expect the best.

SECTION 4

CHECKING
THE EMBERS

The Post-Check

CHECKING THE EMBERS
The Post-Check

Post-Checking Your Reaction to Fear

It is time to stir the embers to see if you have truly doused the Fire of some of your previous responses to your key stressor. You may have felt some relief during the reeducation process as stuck circuits began to unlock. You may have experienced feeling lighter emotionally, a release of tension or pain in your body, more focused and effective. Now we need to reinforce those changes to ensure that they can stand up to a repeat of the initial stressor.

By doing the following Post-Check, you are anchoring into your brain/body your improved neural responses to the issue of fear, creating a new, improved baseline of response. It will give you a conscious awareness of the shift in your neural response to your key issue as a result of our targeted strategies. So let's see if doing the Fire Extinguishers has truly made a difference.

Have a piece of paper and pen ready, and be prepared to jot down any remaining issues that you feel will become priorities for future reeducation efforts. Those who are trained in Muscle Checking can use this process in addition to Noticing[22].

Steps:

1. Have a drink of water, because hydration is essential for brain/body communication.

2. Think of the one specific issue you chose to reeducate in the Pre-Check section on page 37. Imagine it in detail to stimulate more parts of any stuck circuits that may have been formerly fused to it.

3. Now skim through the written Pre-Checks you previously assessed on pages 39–42. Using a different color pencil or pen, evaluate your current brain/body reaction between 0 to 10, and notice which areas have already experienced a change for the better as a result of the Fire Extinguishers. Obviously, long-term behaviors like sleep

patterns etc., will have to be evaluated over the coming days, weeks and months.

4. Doing a Post-Check of your physiological reactions while thinking of your key stressor will give you the satisfaction of detailed, concrete feedback regarding changes in your brain/body response. Please repeat the Noticing process below, while thinking of your stressor.

Noticing How Your Body Acts and Reacts After Brain/Body Balancing

Stand comfortably and, thinking of your key stressor, objectively notice your body responses. This gives you a true measure of any differences achieved as a result of reeducating brain/body communication with the Fire Extinguishers. Afterwards, compare these results with your stressed responses already recorded on pages 43-45, looking for differences and noting improvements.

Notice your posture in relation to the floor. (e.g. upright, swaying forward, backwards or sideways)

_____

Notice any tension, pain or weakness in your body. Where is it? (e.g. legs, back, shoulders, neck, stomach, chest, throat, jaw)

_____

Notice the pace of your heartbeat—slow and steady, or fast.

_____

Notice the pace and depth of your breathing.

_____

Notice if your mouth is moist or dry.

_____

Notice your body temperature. Do some parts of your body feel warm, and others cool?

_____

Notice your emotional state. How are you feeling? Excited, happy, sad, tense, motivated, withdrawn, etc.

_____

Notice your mental state. Can you think clearly or are you confused?

_____

Look at an object straight ahead. Is it clear or blurry?

_____

Listen to a sound in the room. Is it tinny or resonant? Are you hearing equally through both ears?

_____

Lift your straight arms up 30° in front of your body. Is that easy or does it take effort?

_____

Hold your arms there for 30 seconds. Is it easy or difficult?

_____

Jot down what you feel are the most interesting aspects of your body's response after experiencing the Fire Extinguishers:

_____

_____

_____

_____

Compare these results with your stressed responses already recorded on page 43–45 and note the key differences.

_____

_____

_____

_____

If you are still feeling your symptoms of posttraumatic stress disorder at the same intensity as before, and have not noticed any improvements in your physiological signals as a result of these activities, we suggest you seek out professional mental health assistance without delay. If you have Noticed a measurable difference in how you feel and physically respond to your stressor, continue using the reeducation activities you have learned to deepen the new connections.

Establishing a Maintenance Program

Establish a maintenance program so that the positive shifts you have experienced become permanently etched into your neurology. Choose the Fire Extinguishers that feel most effective. If you were aware of an immediate benefit from a particular activity, build it into your self-care. Conversely, also consider those activities which you found most difficult. Repetition of a difficult Fire Extinguisher will myelinate its neural network, creating more efficiency and ease. Chances are, smoothing out the blocks to performing a difficult Fire Extinguisher will be mirrored in easier functioning at everyday tasks that use the same brain/body circuits[23].

> Choose the Fire Extinguishers that feel most effective. Also consider those activities which you found most difficult.

I will use these Stress Releasers to maintain my new integration:

○ 1. Drink Water

○ 2. Plug In for Balanced Energy

○ 3. Cross Patterning

○ 4. Polarized Breathing

○ 5. Cook's Hook-ups

○ 6. Emotional Stress Release (ESR) Points

○ 7. (a) Eye Rotations and/or

○ 7. (b) Affirmations

○ 8. Anchoring

○ 9. Eye Points & Ears

○ 10. Headache Points

○ 11. Fear Tapping Points

○ 12. Leg Muscle Release

○ 13. Sacral Spinal Pump

○ 14. The Energizer

○ 15. Neck and Shoulder Release

○ Other _____

○ Other _____

Number of times a day (3 is average) _____

Number of weeks (at least 3 weeks for habit change) _____

Noticing is a powerful tool to increase your personal awareness and to give you general feedback as to how you are reacting to a given stimulus. However, there is one more valuable tool which can provide you with a deep level body biofeedback—the Muscle Check.

SECTION 5

MORE FIRE-FIGHTING EQUIPMENT

The Muscle Check

MORE FIRE FIGHTING EQUIPMENT
The Muscle Check

Using a Muscle Check for Biofeedback

Although our method of choice for biofeedback to this point has been Noticing, I think there is great value in giving you an experience of direct brain/body communication through a Muscle Check. This will also give you another biofeedback option should you feel comfortable using it.

About 95% of information from our body is unconscious, and the Muscle Check plugs us into this level, providing a stress/no stress read-out directly from the brain and the central nervous system.

Muscles have their own intelligence, and it is profitable to make sure their intelligence is communicating appropriately to the brain.

We have explored how negative emotions—fear in particular—can cause energy blocks and communication imbalances in the body—often manifesting in neurological confusion to the muscles, causing inappropriate tension or weakness. Muscle Checking allows a read-out of over and under energy via a muscle indicator.

> Negative emotions—fear in particular—can cause energy blocks and communication imbalances in the body—often manifesting in neurological confusion to the muscles, causing inappropriate tension or weakness.

With time and practice, you will become very proficient with Muscle Checking. As your skill with Muscle Checking grows, so will your overall body awareness. This awareness is important to have, as it will help guide you to making choices that better support your whole being in your everyday life.

How a muscle communicates

A clear muscle circuit communicates instantly with the brain, holding strong or relaxing as appropriate. For instance, when you step forward on your right leg, your quadriceps muscle, on the front of your thigh, contracts. The hamstring muscle on the back of your leg, relaxes. On your left leg the reverse is happening—hamstring on, and quadriceps relaxed. As the left leg swings forward into the next step, instantly the orders reverse. This is our walking gait—just one of many automatic circuits built in to let us function painlessly and efficiently without thinking about it.

A stressed circuit either cannot stay on, OR cannot shut off. If the messaging gets confused due to stress or trauma, automatic circuits do not fire appropriately, and we tire or experience pain.

Experience brain/muscle communication

Sit in a chair and raise one leg up with the knee bent, lower leg angled 45°, and hold it firm. It is the quadriceps muscle that is raising your leg (actually four muscles in one, hence its name). With your hand, push down on the center of the thigh to see if the muscle is 'on'—able to resist your pressure. Hopefully it is.

1. Sit in a chair and raise one leg up with the knee bent, lower leg angled 45°, and hold it firm.

Now sedate (turn off) the muscle by firmly pinching inward in the belly of the muscle, in the up/down direction of the muscle fibers. Pinch, pinch. Now with your hand push down again on the top of your raised quadriceps with the same pressure as before. Did your muscle release?

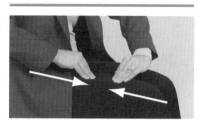

2. *Sedate (turn off) the muscle by firmly pinching inward in the belly of the muscle, in the up/down direction of the muscle fibers.*

In the belly of the muscle are tiny proprioceptors called spindle cells. Their job is to tell the brain whether a muscle is too tight or too relaxed. By pinching the spindle cells closer together, you sent an instantaneous message to the brain, "too close, too close!" and the brain responded with the order to lengthen (relax) the muscle, momentarily turning it off. A normal muscle will reset itself quickly, but experiment with switching the muscle 'on' again.

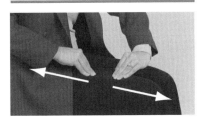

3. Repeat the experiment, but this time, tonify (turn on) the muscle by using your two hands to pull outward from the center of the belly of the muscle, along the direction of the muscle fibers.

Raise your leg once again, your calf angled 45° outward. This time tonify (turn on) the muscle by using your two hands to pull outward from the center of the belly of the muscle, along the direction of the muscle fibers. Once more push down with your hand on the top of your thigh, using the same amount of pressure. Was your muscle able to resist your pressure? You pulled the spindle cells wide apart, and they sent the message "too loose, too loose!" Your brain responded by instantly contracting the muscle, making it strong again.

Congratulations! You have manipulated a muscle and received a functional read-out from the brain and central nervous system—biofeedback via a Muscle Check.

For those who did not get the expected response, have a drink of water, and repeat the process with a stronger pinch and/or a stronger push. If that still does not get the desired response, know that there could be inappropriate messaging from that muscle to the brain. If you want to look into it further, contact a trained kinesiologist or health care professional, as easeful movement is always a by-product of muscles that have clear communication with the brain. A Touch For Health class and/or consulting a licensed health practitioner who manipulates or mobilizes stuck joints can result in a noticeable difference in posture, alignment and performance.

In the same way you checked on the functioning of your quadriceps muscle, you can sedate and tonify other muscles.

> Easeful movement is always a by-product of muscles that have clear communication with the brain. Improving the messaging can result in a noticeable difference in posture, alignment and performance.

Any good anatomy book, and particularly *Touch For Health* by Dr. John Thie, will give you illustrations of the direction of the muscle fibers for you to pinch to relax (great for muscle cramps!) or pull apart (to re-energize). This can give you feedback in regards to the support individual muscles are giving you in any given task. For example, if you were going for a long hike, wouldn't it make sense to assure your quadriceps muscle was 'ready, willing and able'? You can do specific work to reeducate any 'rebels', to help you perform better in any task. As well as helping you reeducate your reaction to stress, you can greatly enhance your golf or tennis game with these techniques!

> When we are injured, the brain sets up pain circuits to remind us not to use the injured area until healed. Our reeducation often releases the unnecessary pain.

The reeducation process often remediates pain. When we are injured, the brain sets up pain circuits to remind us not to use the injured area to give it a chance to heal. Often, after the healing has occurred, the pain circuit remains active, tied into an emotional and mental circuit as well. Once you do some simple brain/body reeducation you can assure the brain that all systems are once again 'go', and that pain is no longer necessary.

Practicing the Muscle Check

If your quadriceps muscle responded appropriately for you in the spindle cell exercise on pages 144–146, your quadriceps muscle is communicating normally with the brain. You can then choose to use the same process to get biofeedback regarding any stressful situation requiring your body's coordination. The intention is that the muscle you are using—the quadriceps—will be an indicator of a whole body response.

In other words, if when you think of a particular stressor, your leg muscle holds its integrity, yet will release when you pinch it in the belly, that stressor is not impacting your body.

If, when you think of a stressor, your leg muscle either falls away, or freezes and is unable to unlock when you pinch it, that issue is causing a stuck circuit lock, and needs to be reeducated with our Fire Extinguishers or another intervention.

Experiment:

1. Have a drink of water, because hydration is essential for brain/body communication.

2. Pre-clear your quadriceps muscle as described on pages 144–146. Your leg should be able to hold strong, yet release when pinched.

3. Think about your key stressor identified in Section 2, page 37.

4. Now, while thinking of that key stressor, choose one of the Pre-Checks we did in Section 2, pages 39–42, which you thought was particularly revealing (a 7–10 rating in your Noticing Pre-Check). Compare your Noticing Post-Check, 0–10, to what you noticed in the Pre-Check. Have you experienced an improvement in your emotional, mental or physical reaction since learning the Fire Extinguishers?

> Have you experienced an improvement in your emotional, mental, or physical reaction to your key stressor?

5. Validate your conscious assessment by adding a Muscle Check. Check your quadriceps muscle as instructed earlier, to see if it holds firm, while still being able to relax when the belly of the muscle is pinched.

If your muscle responds appropriately to what was previously a stressor, and you feel better, you have reeducated your previous reaction to that stressor on a muscle circuit level. If you have a weak or frozen muscle response, you know you still have neurological confusion on that issue, and more reeducation with the Fire Extinguishers is necessary. Repeat your post-test after that reeducation. If you are still experiencing energy blocks, there may be a more complex issue at hand, requiring the assistance of a trained kinesiologist.

> If your muscle responds appropriately, you have reeducated your previous reaction to your key stressor on a muscle circuit level.

Adding a Muscle Check to Noticing

If you feel comfortable that you are getting a useful readout from your brain/body system using this Muscle Checking process, use it following your Noticing procedure. Apply the Muscle Checking procedure pictured on the preceding pages to any of the issues or Pre-Checks on pages 39–42, or any issue you wish to consider in the future[24].

Your Muscle Checking Model

1. Pre-clear that your quadriceps muscle is responding properly. (The muscle is able to resist a pressure, yet relaxes when the belly of the muscle is pinched, and tonifies when the spindle cells are pulled apart.)

2. Think of your stressful situation. Do your conscious Noticing procedure. Jot down the most interesting mental, emotional and physiological markers.

3. Continue to think of your stressor. Lift your leg and lightly resist while pushing down on your thigh. Your quadriceps should be able to hold.   ○ holds   ○ relaxes

4. Pinch in belly of muscle, and push down on thigh again. The muscle should relax.   ○ holds   ○ relaxes

5. Pull apart in belly of muscle and Muscle Check again. The muscle should reset and be strong once more.   ○ holds   ○ relaxes

    ○ Muscle responds appropriately

    ○ Does not hold strong when appropriate

    ○ Does not relax when appropriate

If the muscle does not respond appropriately, you must reeducate the stress response, and recheck later to anchor in improvements.

A Muscle Check, with its stress/no stress readout from deep in the nervous system, will often surprise you by telling a very different story from what you consciously feel and think regarding your Pre-Checks and Post-Checks. Remain open and curious as to the response, and approach the Muscle Check without any specific expectation. Further training in Muscle Checking will expand your understanding and skills[25]. With this training, the Muscle Check can be used to help determine which Fire Extinguishers would be the most effective to use for your Maintenance Program, and to pinpoint which priority stress trigger you should address next .

SECTION 6

OTHER BURNING ISSUES

Sources of Stress in Your Everyday Life

OTHER BURNING ISSUES
Sources of Stress in Your
Everyday Life

Now that you have begun building your immunity to stress, it is time to:

1) Gain a more in-depth understanding of what stress is beyond the emotional factors, and how it impacts your well-being

2) Become more consciously aware of the specific obstacles (external and internal life stressors) that are hampering you in your life, and

3) Explore varied options to start handling them immediately.

The Continuum of Well-Being

Think of well-being as a continuum. At 0% you are dead, and at 100% you are brimming with vitality and have a large reservoir of adaptive ability to handle stress. We all fall somewhere on the continuum, with mental, physical and emotional wear and tear starting to show when we fall below 50%. We may wake up in the morning feeling great, but in truth we may be just one sleepless night, and two cups of coffee away from experiencing mental, physical, or emotional symptoms of imbalance.

> These external substances mimic our natural 'feel-good' biochemicals, bind to our brain's receptors, and depress our body's ability to manufacture our own positive chemical messengers.

Our brain/body's desire to maintain an emotionally buoyant state has long drawn us to look for the immediate, synthetic state change triggered by a pill, a drink, a sugar lift or a caffeine jolt. For instance, chocolate contains phenylalanine which triggers release of oxytocin, the same 'bliss, cuddle and bonding' neurotransmitter generated when we fall in love, or have a child. No wonder so many of us crave chocolate when we are stressed!

These external substances mimic our natural 'feel-good' biochemicals, bind to our brain's receptors, and depress our body's ability to manufacture our own positive chemical messengers. They can mask our awareness of our true position on the wellness continuum.

Insight: Where do you feel you are on the continuum of well-being?

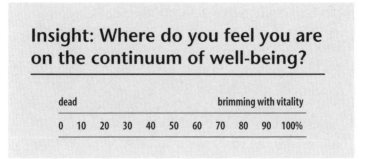

dead									brimming with vitality	
0	10	20	30	40	50	60	70	80	90	100%

Some theorists believe that this is the aging process: Constant straining against life events places us in the classic stress response cycle; we destroy our immune system, fall victim to opportunistic disease, experience physical wear and tear, and die. Therefore, genetic inheritance being equal, we can control mental, emotional and physical wear and tear as well as aging, by learning adaptive skills to conserve our stress 'shield' and build up our resources.

What is Stress?

The only sure thing in our world is constant change, and anything—be it good or bad—that requires the body to spend precious energy adapting is 'Stress.' Theoretically everything that makes the slightest impression on us, causing us to process new information—from the touch of a child's hand, to a car accident—is a stressor. A wedding or winning the lottery can be as stressful (though more pleasurable) than being fired or divorced. Remember that it is the emotional filter through which we perceive an event that gives the event its label as good, bad or indifferent, and determines the intensity of its impact.

So stress itself is not the enemy. Actually sensory stimulation is a 'Good Guy' as it leads to learning, the layering of improved neural (nerve/muscle) connections in the brain and body, and positive action. Good stress was called 'eustress' by Dr. Hans Selye, the father of modern stress theory.

The 'Bad Guy' is 'distress', unresolved stress response. The strain of ineffectively dealing with our reality leads to short circuits in the body's normal electrical communication. In this book we have termed this the 'Fire'.

Winning the lottery can be as stressful (though more pleasurable) than being fired or divorced.

Distress (strain) is caused by inadequate coping mechanisms in response to the obstacles (stressors) with which we must all deal in daily life.

A Closer Look at the Pot of Stress

To help you get a better understanding of what your ongoing stressors are, we invite you to take a closer look at your pot of stress on the next page. Identifying and neutralizing seemingly unrelated areas of stress in your life will improve your overall functioning.

Identifying and neutralizing seemingly unrelated areas of stress in your life will improve your overall functioning.

Bottom line: Stress accumulates. All your stressors go into one pot to assault your body's resources. So it pays to identify and neutralize little, as well as big life issues. Remember, it's almost always a 'little' thing that is the last straw, throwing us into dysfunctional imbalance.

What's In Your Pot of Stress?[26]

Check the boxes which identify the key stressors in your life. Which ones can you remove, reduce or reeducate?

Emotional

- ○ Past Emotional Trauma
- ○ Current & Future Worries & Anxieties
- ○ Fears & Phobias
- ○ Lack of Spiritual Awareness/ Religious Faith
- ○ Fear of Failure and/or Success
- ○ Past Programming

Physical

- ○ Musculoskeletal Stress
- ○ Inappropriate Exercise
- ○ Poor Posture
- ○ Maladjustment to Workplace
- ○ Shallow Breathing

Environmental

- ○ Sensitivity to Fluorescent Lighting
- ○ Sensitivity/Allergy to Specific Colors
- ○ Sensitivity to Noise
- ○ Radiation and Electromagnetic Pollution (effects in this area are subtle, often unrecognized and cumulative)

Behavioral

- ○ Inadequate Sleep and Rest
- ○ Use/Abuse of 'Recreational' & Medicinal Drugs
- ○ Dysfunctional Family Background
- ○ Perfectionism
- ○ Procrastination
- ○ Workaholism
- ○ Lack of Time Management & Organizational Skills

Chemical

- ○ Insufficient Water Intake
- ○ Poor Dietary Choices
- ○ Nutritional Deficiencies
- ○ Food and/or Environmental Allergies (sensitivities)
- ○ Heavy Metal Toxicity
- ○ Impure Air and Water
- ○ Agricultural Sprays

A kick in the rear can cause a pain in the head

We humans are not simply machines; we are mental, emotional, spiritual, as well as biochemical and physical beings. A blow to any of these areas impacts the equilibrium of our whole. When we experience a symptom (imbalance), it has not necessarily been triggered by an obvious stressor (cause and effect). For instance, our back may go out, not because we lifted a box the wrong way, but because we had a fight with our spouse and our back is our weakest link. A person may eat biochemically stressful foods and not understand why he is always depressed. Another may be in a car accident without physical injury, only to break out in an allergic rash... and so it goes.

An emotional stressor (like a fight with your spouse) can cause physical symptoms.

All the professional attention in the world won't give us permanent relief from our diverse symptoms unless we also identify and relieve the major (often seemingly unrelated) causal stressors.

What is your 'Achilles Heel'?

Remember the Greek myth of Achilles? He was invincible, except for the heel by which he was held when dipped for invulnerability into the waters of the Styx. He was eventually killed by a poisoned arrow striking that one vulnerable spot.

So take a hard look at your weakest link—your recurring physical or behavioral symptom. Whatever it is—allergy, depression, sore back, weak stomach, etc., know that it is a combination of all life stressors that has caused you to experience that symptom. For an improvement that holds, you must ultimately look beyond the straight-line cause and effect, to restore balance and well-being to your overall brain/body system.

INSIGHT: My Weakest Link

What's your weakest link? Scan the Pre-Check Lists you completed on pages 39-42 for additional insights.

Emotional

◯ Fear   ◯ Anxiety   ◯ Easily irritated

◯ Depression   ◯ Other _____

Physical

◯ Chronic pain   ◯ Bad back   ◯ Headaches   ◯ Flu

◯ Rash   ◯ Allergy   ◯ Other _____

Mental

◯ Loss of focus and concentration   ◯ Loss of productivity

◯ Forgetfulness   ◯ Other _____

Behavioral

◯ Negative changes in personal habits

       (e.g., ◯ eating,   ◯ drinking,

              ◯ smoking   ◯ recreational or prescription drugs)

◯ Work habits

◯ Other _____

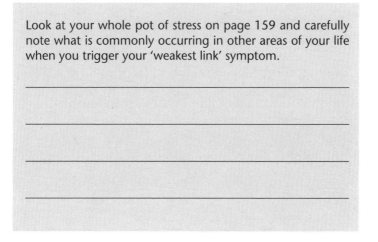

Look at your whole pot of stress on page 159 and carefully note what is commonly occurring in other areas of your life when you trigger your 'weakest link' symptom.

A Quick Detour to Goal Setting

Before going any further, it makes sense to take a slight detour to look at your goals. This will help clarify which stressors don't serve your long-term purpose, and will aid you in your decision process of what goes, and what stays.

Most people are so busy treading water, they're not clear in what direction they should be swimming. Particularly today when the present seems overwhelming, it is hard for many to look to the future. How can you hope to get where you're going if you don't know where you're heading? This book is intended to 'clear the decks' to get you into a state where it is possible to look beyond survival to productive personal change.

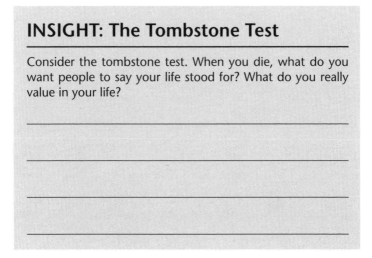

Most conventional books on Stress Management emphasize detailed assessment of your goals. If you are familiar with goal setting, we recommend you review your goals as soon as you finish this book[27].

In consideration of any goals you have already established, or at the very least your Tombstone Test, above, start identifying all the stressors that don't support your life purpose. Be ruthless in eliminating irrelevant stressors, non-serving relationships, and expectations. Use the stress management techniques you have acquired to make it easy to do so without guilt. Use the Three R's model on the next page to help you get started.

The Three R's for Managing Stress:

1. Remove

(a) the stressor: Eliminate any of the stressors you've defined in your pot of stress on page 159), or life pressures that are adding to the existing stress load you have defined on the previous page. Example: Clean up your messy desk.

(b) yourself from the stressor: Close the door so you don't have to look at the desk (or change jobs, if that's the stressor).

2. Reduce

the stressor: Buy some new organizers for your desk; organize your schedule to give yourself more time to tidy up; throw away unneeded papers; reduce clutter.

3. Reeducate

your brain/body response, so your buttons aren't pushed every time you look at the desk, throwing you into overwhelm.

Remove or modify the 'small time' stressors that are on your plate. Each one may be little, but in accumulation they become a tremendous load, and use up the stress resilience you need to cope with the unavoidable major stressors in everyday life.

Take a look at everything demanding your time and attention. Does it support your life and goals? Are you having any fun? If not, look closely at the ways you are sabotaging and depleting yourself. Take a moment to consider some first steps toward lightening your pot of stress, and getting out of survival mode.

In the insight activity that follows, identify issues you are immediately willing to address. It can be as simple as drinking 1 cup of coffee less per day. Then follow through and remove, reduce and/or reeducate them in the weeks ahead.

INSIGHT: Your Choices for Removing, Reducing or Reeducating Stress

List at least two stressors in each category you are willing to address using the three 'R's:

Remove a) the stressor

1. _____   2. _____

Remove b) yourself

1. _____   2. _____

Reduce the stressor

1. _____   2. _____

Reeducate your mental, physiological or emotional response to

1. _____

2. _____

How to Address Your Burning Issues

The next section will give you an easy model to follow as you attend to the list you just made. By using integrating activities from this point forward, not only can you defuse currently stuck stress circuits, but you are also less likely to lock in new negative stress circuits. The buildup of your negative pot of stress can stop right here and now. It's up to you to choose to use the tools you have acquired. Here's a simple model to help you extinguish the other burning issues in your life.

SECTION 7

PUTTING OUT EVERYDAY FIRES

Applying the Model to Your Life

PUTTING OUT EVERYDAY FIRES
Applying the Model to Your Life

Using Your Fire Extinguishers the Simplest Way

Take these individual activities with you into your real life, adapting them to fit into your home and work environments. The most important thing to remember is 'an ounce of prevention is worth a pound of cure'. The best way to put out a forest fire would be when the first spark ignites. So too, as soon as you notice the first sign of a stress response in your system, you should stop in your tracks right then and there (or as soon as it is safe to do so). Immediately reeducate the non-serving stress symptom, then go back to your activity, noticing if you are functioning at a higher level. In so doing you are actively applying the model of the information sandwich to your everyday life:

Top slice: (Pre-Check), Noticing wherever functioning is sub-optimal.

Filling: (Reeducate) with the 'Quick Six' or individual Fire Extinguishers

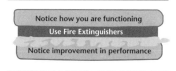

Bottom Slice: (Post-Check) to see you are now functioning and feeling better.

Mission accomplished in maintaining a calm, balanced state.

The 'Quick Six' in Everyday Life

At the end of many of our activities in Section 3, we gave you Variations in Real Life—how to use the Fire Extinguishers in public places without being noticed. Let's review the 'Quick Six'—the very minimum support for whole brain/body functioning.

Always keep a water glass or bottle handy, for little sips throughout the day. As soon as you start to feel fuzzy-brained, take a sip of water, take a deep breath, and reach up with one hand to casually massage your 'plugging in' energy points (page 66), first on one side of your breastbone, then the other. From time to time, reach up and massage your eye points (page 111), first one side, then the other. Do the same for your ears, casually massaging one, then later, the other (page 113). As mentioned earlier, the worst thing that can happen is that people will think you are itchy. No one will know you are constantly maintaining your immunity to stress with superb body management skills.

> The 'Quick Six' are a great support for whole-brain functioning and a balanced energy state. You can adapt them to fit unobtrusively into your everyday life.

You can do the Cross Patterning activity (page 74) unobtrusively anywhere—in a waiting room, an exam, a meeting—reactivating your brain hemispheres by simply flicking an opposite finger and toe, using minute movements. Your brain is firing off the circuits for brain/body integration, even without big gestures.

Modify your Cook's Hook-up (page 83), by comfortably crossing your arms and legs, without actually grasping the ball of your foot. Nobody knows your tongue is on the roof of your mouth. Then, do the second part—feet flat on the floor, and fingertips together. People use this method all the time. It's an instinctive stance for energy balancing and stress release.

The same is true for the Emotional Stress Release posture of hand placed lightly on the forehead (page 88). People do this instinctively all the time. All we have to remember is to do it deliberately, and to hold our hand in place. It's easy when we're seated at a desk or table. As already advised, write tests or work to deadline with one hand on your forehead.

Always respond to your system's stress signals as soon as you become aware of them. Then maintain your gains by using the 'Quick Six' regularly. This is the simplest way of working with the tools—just choosing individual activities you like to rebalance yourself the moment you notice you are not functioning optimally, or to prepare for the next challenge.

> Always respond to your system's stress signals as soon as you become aware of them, with a Fire Extinguisher. Then, maintain your gains by using the 'Quick Six' regularly.

Over time you will notice that your reaction to stress will become less intense and more proactive. With your new skills you will have built up your immunity to stress.

A Simple Model to Work on Any Issue or Goal[28]

The next step is for you to choose to embark on a deliberate reeducation of your brain/body system for a specific task or issue.

It's very much like tidying up the house[29]. Once you are no longer tripping over things on the floor in the main rooms, you can deliberately open the cupboard doors and clean out your messy closets. Similarly, once you have the issues that have been negatively impacting you daily under control, you can attend to older, more hidden issues which although stressful, have perhaps been ignored.

Here is an outline of the steps we will be taking:

1. Set the goal.

2. Pre-Check (The Information Sandwich Top Slice): Notice the resources and brain/body response you currently bring to that goal or stressful situation.

3. Reeducate (The Information Sandwich Filling): Your brain/body response with our Fire Extinguishers.

4. Post-Check (The Information Sandwich Bottom Slice): Notice improvements in your brain/body functioning in regard to that goal or formerly stressful situation.

5. Set a maintenance plan to support your new-found integration.

1. Setting The Goal

Do you already know your next goal? Fill it in here, and proceed immediately to the Pre-Checks at number 2.

My goal or the priority stress response I wish to reeducate is:

_____

If you are not clear on which goal or stressful situation to choose, consider the following possibilities:

What do you consider your major stressors?

○ World Situation ○ Fears as listed on page 36

○ Parents   ○ Spouse   ○ Children

○ Bills   ○ No time and too much to do

○ Other _____

○ Other _____

○ Other _____

Refer back to page 159 for issues from your Pot of Stress.

_____

_____

Refer back to your choices for Removing, Reducing or Reeducating Stress on page 167. Create your fresh insight list here:

What stressors I am willing to:

Remove

1. _____   2. _____

Reduce

1. _____   2. _____

Reeducate

1. _____   2. _____

From all of the above, choose your next key stressor now.

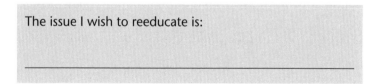

The issue I wish to reeducate is:

_____

2. The Pre-Check

Written Pre-Check

I am aware of experiencing symptoms of stress in the following areas (refer back to your Pre-Checks on pages 39–42 if desired):

Emotional

○ Anxiety   ○ Irritability   ○ Depression

Mental

○ Fatigue   ○ Overcompensation   ○ Denial

Behavioral

○ Avoidance   ○ Extreme Mood Swings

○ Problems handling my:

  ○ Life   ○ Work   ○ Relationships

Physical

○ Frequent Illness   ○ Exhaustion   ○ Self-Medication

Other

○ _____

○ _____

○ _____

Physiological Pre-Check

INSIGHT: Noticing Your Physiological Reactions To Your Stressor

Keeping in mind your chosen issue or challenging situation, do this Noticing process. Stand comfortably and objectively Notice your body responses. Jot down the most interesting mental, emotional and physiological markers. Compare your findings against your established baseline for a relaxed state on pages 31–33.

Notice your posture in relation to the floor. (e.g. upright, swaying forward, backwards or sideways)

_____

Notice any tension, pain or weakness in your body. Where is it? (e.g. legs, back, shoulders, neck, stomach, chest, throat, jaw)

_____

Notice the pace of your heartbeat—slow and steady, or fast.

_____

Notice the pace and depth of your breathing.

_____

Notice if your mouth is moist or dry.

_____

Notice your body temperature: Do some parts of your body feel warm, and others cool?

Notice your emotional state. How are you feeling? Excited, happy, sad, tense, motivated, withdrawn, etc.

Notice your mental state. Can you think clearly or are you confused?

Look at an object straight ahead. Is it clear or blurry?

Listen to a sound in the room. Is it tinny or resonant? Are you hearing equally through both ears?

Lift your straight arms up 30° in front of your body. Is that easy or does it take effort?

Hold your arms there for 30 seconds. Is it easy or difficult?

Compare these results with your relaxed baseline responses already recorded on page 31-33 and note the key differences.

_____

_____

_____

_____

If you choose, add a Muscle Check to Noticing:

Your Muscle Checking Model

If any of these checks are different from the expected normal response, this means that neurological confusion in your muscle has occurred because of stress associated with your challenge.

1. Pre-Check that your quadriceps muscle is responding properly. (The muscle is able to resist a pressure, yet relaxes when the belly of the muscle is pinched, and tonifies when the spindle cells are pulled apart.)

2. Think of your stressful situa-   ○ holds   ○ relaxes
   tion. Lift your leg and lightly
   resist while pushing down on
   your thigh. Your quadriceps
   should be able to hold.

3. Pinch in belly of muscle, and push down on thigh again. The muscle should relax.

○ holds   ○ relaxes

4. Pull apart in belly of muscle and Muscle Check again. The muscle should reset and be strong once more.

○ holds   ○ relaxes

Note Differences:

○ Muscle responds appropriately

○ Does not hold strong when appropriate

○ Does not relax when appropriate

If the muscle does not respond appropriately, you must reeducate the stress response, and recheck later to anchor in improvements.

3. The Filling: Reeducating the Brain/ Body Response

Choose one or all of the following of groups A, B, C or D:

A. *Choose your favorite Fire Extinguisher(s)*

○ 1. Drink Water

○ 2. Plug In for Balanced Energy

○ 3. Cross Patterning

○ 4. Polarized Breathing

○ 5. Cook's Hook-ups

○ 6. Emotional Stress Release (ESR) Points

○ 7. (a) Eye Rotations and/or

○ 7. (b) Affirmations

○ 8. Anchoring

○ 9. Eye Points & Ears

○ 10. Headache Points

○ 11. Fear Tapping Points

○ 12. Leg Muscle Release

○ 13. Sacral Spinal Pump

○ 14. The Energizer

○ 15. Neck and Shoulder Release

○ Other _____

○ Other _____

B. The 'Quick Six'

1. Drink Water
(page 63)

**2. Plugging In For Balanced
Energy** (page 66)

3. Cross Patterning
(page 71)

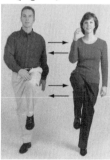

4. Cook's Hook-ups
(page 83)

6. Be Sense-able
(page 111, 113)

**5. Emotional Stress
Release** (page 88)

C. PACE™ Process from Brain Gym®

Brain Buttons™
(page 68)

3. Active

2. Clear

1. Energetic

Drink Water
(page 63)

4. Positive

Cross Crawl
(page 75)

Hook-ups™
(page 84)

Each person has a unique and appropriate pace for optimal learning and functioning. In the Educational Kinesiology model, we PACE™ [30] ourselves regularly with these four Brain Gym® activities in order to maintain an optimal state of mind/body coherence. Begin with water, and notice your responses, anchoring improvement as you proceed.

D. *Other activities of my own choosing:*

_____

_____

_____

4. Post-Check

Noticing How Your Body Acts and Reacts After Brain/Body Balancing

Stand comfortably and, thinking of your key stressor, objectively notice your body responses. This gives you a true measure of any differences achieved as a result of reeducating brain/body communication with the Fire Extinguishers. Afterwards, compare these results with your stressed responses already recorded on pages 178–180, looking for differences and noting improvements.

Notice your posture in relation to the floor. (e.g. upright, swaying forward, backwards or sideways)

_____

Notice any tension, pain or weakness in your body. Where is it? (e.g. legs, back, shoulders, neck, stomach, chest, throat, jaw)

_____

Notice the pace of your heartbeat—slow and steady, or fast.

_____

Notice the pace and depth of your breathing.

_____

Notice if your mouth is moist or dry.

_____

Notice your body temperature: Do some parts of your body feel warm, and others cool?

_____

Notice your emotional state. How are you feeling? Excited, happy, sad, tense, motivated, withdrawn, etc.

_____

Notice your mental state. Can you think clearly or are you confused?

_____

Look at an object straight ahead. Is it clear or blurry?

_____

Listen to a sound in the room. Is it tinny or resonant? Are you hearing equally through both ears?

_____

Lift your straight arms up 30° in front of your body. Is that easy or does it take effort?

_____

Hold your arms there for 30 seconds. Is it easy or difficult?

_____

Jot down the most interesting aspects of your body's response to reeducation with the Fire Extinguishers, as compared to your stressed reactions on pages 178–180. Note improvements. If there are any imbalances that you feel require more attention, continue with more Fire Extinguishers or other processes.

_____

_____

_____

_____

If you are satisfied with the level of improvement in your brain/body response, you are done, and can choose to support your new level of processing with the following maintenance program.

5. My Maintenance Program

To support my new ease in regards to my key issue, I will use these Stress Releasers to maintain my new integration:

○ 1. Drink Water	○ 10. Headache Points
○ 2. Plug In for Balanced Energy	○ 11. Fear Tapping Points
○ 3. Cross Patterning	○ 12. Leg Muscle Release
○ 4. Polarized Breathing	○ 13. Sacral Spinal Pump
○ 5. Cook's Hook-ups	○ 14. The Energizer
○ 6. Emotional Stress Release (ESR) Points	○ 15. Neck and Shoulder Release
	○ 16. Quick Six
○ 7. (a) Eye Rotations and/or	○ 17. PACE™
○ 7. (b) Affirmations	○ Other _____
○ 8. Anchoring	○ Other _____
○ 9. Eye Points & Ears	

Number of times a day (3 is average) _____

Number of weeks (at least 3 weeks for habit change) _____

I will incorporate other simple stress strategies into my everyday planning (see pages 190–194 for ideas):

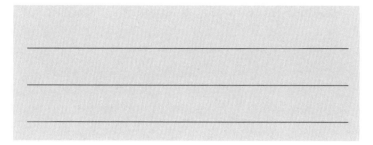

Once you are satisfied that you have reeducated and anchored your brain/body response to your former stressor, and when you feel ready, identify the next priority stressor or issue that you wish to address. It may be a specific issue upon which you have already touched, a stressor you identified earlier in your Pot of Stress, or a challenge from your everyday life. You now have the rhythm of the model, and can apply it to improve any issue.

The intention is for you to slowly chip away at removing your ongoing stressors. Your ultimate goal is to clear out as many unnecessary drains on your life energy as is feasible, and then to reeducate your reaction to the stressors that remain. The tools in this book will help you to accomplish this. Rather than being controlled by your stress response, you can remain calm, front-brained and fully functional as you move forward in your life, even in a threatening world.

What Else Can You Do?

Naturally there are all the conventional ways of managing stress, such as joining a fitness club, taking a hot bath, meditating, or a thousand and one methods that might work for you. Hundreds of books and articles have been written on the subject. To get you started, here are some basic suggestions drawn from the Canadian Mental Health Association. We have already taken you in detail through the first two most important ones.

Everyday stress releasers[31]

1. Recognize your symptoms of stress.

2. Look at your life-style and see what can be changed—in your work situation, your family situation, or your schedule.

3. Use relaxation techniques—yoga, mediation, deep breathing, or massage.

4. Exercise: Physical activity is one of the most effective stress remedies around!

5. Time management: Do essential tasks and prioritize the others. Be sure to consider those who may be affected by your decisions, such as family and friends. Use a checklist so you will receive satisfaction as you check off each job as it is done.

6. Watch your diet: Alcohol, caffeine, sugar, fats and tobacco all put a strain on your body's abil-

ity to cope with stress. A diet with a balance of fruits, vegetables, whole grains and foods high in protein but low in fat will help create optimum health. Contact your local chapter of the Heart and Stroke Foundation for further information about healthy eating.

7. Get enough rest and sleep.

8. Talk with others: Talk with friends, professional counselors, support groups or relatives about what is bothering you.

9. Help others: Volunteer work can be an effective and satisfying stress reducer.

10. Get away for a while: Read a book, watch a movie, play a game, listen to music or go on vacation. Leave yourself some time that's just for you.

11. Work off your anger: Get physically active, dig in the garden, start a project, get your spring-cleaning done.

12. Give in occasionally: Avoid quarrels whenever possible. (In other words, choose your battles carefully—make sure it's an important issue before you dig in.)

13. Tackle one thing at a time: Don't try to do too much at once.

14. Don't try to be perfect.

15. Ease up on criticism of others.

16. Don't be too competitive.

17. Make the first move to be friendly.

18. Have some fun! Laugh and be with people you enjoy.

To this list I add:

19. Use Positive Self-talk: Reframe Negativity.

You always have a choice: Are you going to allow yourself to be stressed by an event, or are you going to reframe the experience and learn from it? As an example, next time you are listening to a boring presentation, speech or sermon (and leaving is not an option), you have a choice. You can get anxious, upset, stressed, restless and impatient, or you can reframe the experience. Consider it a role-play of what you must never do as a teacher/speaker. Consciously analyzing an example of what not to do, can be even more valuable than a sample of good presenting.

Here's another relevant example for those of us who work with a computer: If you lose some work through hitting a wrong key or a systems crash, reframe the experience. Think: "How can I be even clearer and simpler in my communication?" (I know that I have often done better in my second version after losing my first draft.) Another of my personal experiences has been to consider it a lucky break that the whole project was not lost when the system crashed, and to take it as a sign to buy a file retrieval program and to have a backup system working regularly before more serious loss can happen.

20. Break Your Addiction to Television and the News.

An important tip from mental health professionals is to break our harmful addiction to the news. It is in the media's self-interest to create viewership and thus more revenue dollars. We are often exposed to sensationalism and have horrific images repetitively thrust into our consciousness in the name of keeping us informed. It is in our best interest to resist the survival triggers the media use to keep us riveted through the next commercial break. Have you ever noticed how often the interesting story that is the teaser "coming up after...", is the last one of the broadcast? This ploy puts us in the Alarm 'full alert' stage of stress, leaving us unable to easily break away until we know it is safe to do so and/or until our curiosity is satisfied. Why not hold your Emotional Stress Release Points while you take in the news? Another suggestion is not to watch the late news as you prepare for bed. Obviously you are inviting sleep problems if your last conscious thoughts and images of the day are disturbing.

With the issue of children and TV, there are three concerns. First, we must protect our children from the desensitization of the violence shown every day in the media[32].

Second, the electromagnetic impulse from the screen itself constitutes a stressor on human electromagnetic brain/body energy, as it is a conflicting frequency. Some studies suggest television viewing can seriously impede brain, visual and language development in young children[33].

Third, the time children spend sitting before a TV or computer screen is time not spent moving and playing, which are so essential for their motor and brain development. The same holds true for adults. Moderation is essential in regard to television viewing, the same way it is the smart choice regarding other stressors we might enjoy, like coffee or chocolate cake.

In Conclusion

If we want to help our body attain and maintain a state of emotional, physical and mental well-being, it makes sense for us to moderate the stressors in our lives; eat right, sleep right, manage our time, exercise, and definitely, as this book instructs, do the Fire Extinguishers. They are designed to give our system a chance to naturally manufacture and regulate the appropriate biochemicals necessary for a balanced emotional state. You can also build in any other brain/body balancing modalities you know into your self-care program.

That doesn't mean you can be expected to do it all in one day. Choose which of the above suggestions, and which of our Fire Extinguishers, to build into your life right away. Add more as you choose. The only thing you shouldn't choose, is to do nothing! Remember, inactivity does not help the stress hormones to dissipate, and it locks you into an ever-escalating stress response.

A motto I have up on my wall reads "Improve 1% a day". This is a doable goal. It also means that by the end of several months, you will be unrecognizable in your ability to handle your life and in your personal effectiveness. I invite you to make that commitment to improve 1% a day, and Notice the difference these simple concepts and activities will make in your life.

SECTION 8

ADDENDA

Stress From the Brain's Point of View

Current brain research is giving us valuable information on what actually transpires in the brain when we are stressed. Much of this research has the intention of determining how to medically balance the release/inhibition cycles of the neurotransmitters and hormones that control the stress response[34]. The premise of this book is that the simple brain/ body interventions to which you have been introduced may help you to naturally control your stress response, and should be fully explored rather than simply resorting to medication.

In the introduction to our book we touched upon how, to be optimally functional, the brain and the rest of the body must be in clear communication. Information must be able to flow freely and instantaneously from the body to specific areas of the brain and back again, and from brain part to brain part, each operating separately and as a part of the whole.

Current research is shaking up our concepts of the nature of emotion and where it lives, expanding it to a cellular level throughout the body. Of great interest is the work of neuroscientist Candace Pert, Ph.D., discoverer of the opiate receptor, who describes neuropeptides that travel in a secondary free-floating nervous system like the endocrine system, as 'the molecules of emotion'[35]. The emotional 'brain' is no longer confined to the classic location of the midbrain, even though the midbrain is largely responsible for interpreting and processing that emotion. According to Pert, there are other hot spots throughout the body, particularly where the five senses enter the nervous system[36]. Pert has even insightfully referred to the body as the 'unconscious mind'[37].

Information feeds in from the world via our proprioceptive and sensory receptors, and feeds into the brain, first passing from the spinal column into the brain stem. The Reticular Activating System (or RAS) is the arousal sentry. It wakes up the brain to all incoming signals, and filters out nonessential information. The RAS acts as a toggle switch that opens and shuts access to higher critical reasoning (it has axons reaching up into the lower reaches of the cortex), based on whether the midbrain (with its emotional centers) is relaxed. The RAS stands on guard to see if we are under attack, in which case signals are diverted immediately to the automatic survival and action centers of the brain, and amongst other responses, the tendon guard reflex is triggered.

If the RAS feels it is safe to do so, (and the information is interesting enough to warrant attention), the information moves upward to the midbrain, where it must pass a second sentry, the Amygdala, to determine our ultimate response. This brain part helps regulate emotion. It loves excitement and novelty. If the Amygdala finds the information interesting and safe (even if exciting), the signals can proceed up into the cerebral cortex for further analysis, new ideas, plan making and new action. However, if the Amygdala has interpreted the signals as deserving attention, but potentially dangerous, it diverts the information immediately back to the automatic survival centers. The action is once again determined by the old tapes of the cerebellum: How

SIMPLE BRAIN ANATOMY

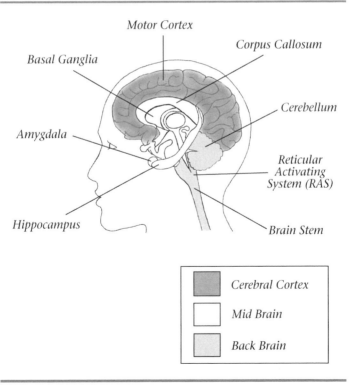

did you react before? New, more effective solutions are not possible—just old survival responses. The additional bad news is that with the back-brained stress response in full swing, we revert to a dominant brain organization profile, losing much of the processing power of our non-dominant brain hemisphere, and our non-dominant eye, ear, and hand. We are losing out on much of the detail or the big picture when this happens.

Meanwhile, back at the Amygdala: the Amygdala also helps a brain part called the Hippocampus decide what gets layered into long term memory. Emotion is the key. The stronger the emotion, positive or negative, the stronger the imprint on the memory systems of the body, both conscious and cellular. The danger signals that have become intertwined with our concept of fear elicit automatic protective reactions in situations that formerly were neutral, and become etched in stone until such time as the circuits are defused.

Have you ever wondered how a thought gets turned into physical action? Think of raising your arm. Now do it. How did you do that? After consciously deciding on a plan of action in the frontal areas of the cerebral cortex, the orders for intentional physical action get sent out by brain parts called the basal ganglia, to the motor cortex for new movement. The basal ganglia are integral to that magical transmutation of thought into action. When you have learned to do something automatically, like walking, the action is overseen by the automatic back brain (cerebellum). As soon as you are alerted to new information, like a car approaching, the basal ganglia and higher brain takes over to make safety adjustments to your action.

The bottom line: If you don't satisfy the safety needs of your lower brain stem and the Amygdala, you cannot have the processing power of your whole brain to be calm, controlled and at your best. You can't get the basal ganglia to send out new orders on how to behave differently in what has become locked in as an automatic situation. You also won't be able to halt the biochemical mechanism, and the stress response will escalate.

If the Fire of Fear has you locked into set reactions (like many traumatized New Yorkers fearful of riding on the subway, being in tall buildings, or even on the street), you must satisfy your brain that it can let go of that learned traumatic lesson of survival. How will you satisfy these brain parts that it's safe to react differently in the face of a traumatic stress trigger?

How can you satisfy the brain's requiring a sense of safety? The activities in this book help you achieve a return to a non-stressed homeostasis, by providing patterned, targeted activities that activate the brain wave state experienced in a state of relaxation and safety. The Fire Extinguishers, as described earlier, actually stimulate the release of positive neurotransmitters, re-educate the stress response, and thus create within you your own personal safety zone. In cases of Attention Deficit Disorder, they give the brain/body system a framework around which it can reorganize itself back into a coherent state. You owe it to yourself to give them a chance to help you regain that state of self-control and well-being which allows you to move through the world both relaxed and alert.

Ritual can also provide the human brain an important link to familiarity and safety. The role of ritual in our lives deserves to be touched upon. In times of stress, ritual can be a supportive tool for stress release. If carried to extremes, it can be a marker of dysfunction.

The Nature of Ritual

All the major religions and energy disciplines are built upon a framework of ritual, which is very satisfying to the brain. Through multisensory stimuli—action, sight, sound, smell, location—rituals trigger a desired, remembered state. Used both to energize or to calm, these stimuli include smells that trigger comforting childhood memories, familiar songs that access a deep comforting sense of community and belonging, body postures that actually help the body conduct its energy circuits more smoothly. For example, the common prayer posture with the fingertips of both hands together, is actually extremely balancing on an energetic level.

Rituals/habits can also serve as touchstones to tell us that something significant is happening. They help us instill meaning into our world. We create rituals for beginnings and endings. We come together in our humanity to create rites of passage—ceremonies celebrating birth, weddings and other joyous occasions, and again to memorialize death. These traditions provide a framework that is very cathartic to the human condition. Some of these rituals are designed to arouse, rather than calm—just think of the running of the bulls in Pamplona, Spain, or the Mardi Gras in New Orleans. We have festivals of joy before periods of self-examination: We have holidays of light, to push back the darkness. There is a rhythm to ritual.

Small rituals provide comfort as well as large ones. If every action required conscious thought and a new decision, we would be overwhelmed just getting out the door in the morning. We create rituals (routines) around rising and bedtime. There is a comfort in automatic habit, and family traditions.

For those of you who may not have many rituals built into your life, you may find that the stress releasers you have learned can help fill that gap. They will provide you with a nurturing 'time out' to stop an automatic stress response. Used regularly, they create a bridge to more positive functioning and reinforcement of your new brain circuitry. They provide an easy way for you to create the balanced energy state which is interpreted by your brain as 'safety'. They facilitate the unimpeded flow of information through the brain stem, the Reticular Activating System, the midbrain and the Amygdala, to your higher reasoning cortex for new planning and ideas.

What positive traditions or habits do you currently have in your life that help you feel safe and in control? They can be habits of self-care and nurturing—a few minutes for calm and quiet enjoyment in a busy day. Or they can be family traditions that bring you together and give you a sense of belonging with loved ones.

INSIGHT: My current positive traditions and habits

1. _____

2. _____

3. _____

To these, add a new ritual:

4. As soon as I notice an inappropriate stress response, I will use a Fire Extinguisher to return to a balanced state.

Other habits/traditions I can add:

5. _____

6. _____

If you have no family, it's particularly important to seek out community via a religious institution, support group or special interest group. Create habits of service to your community. This gives you the satisfaction of knowing that you have made a difference, and that you have a secure place where you are valued. Whenever you volunteer, you gain as much—or more—than you give.

THE OTHER EXTREMES ON THE CONTINUUM

We must always keep in mind that ritual is meant to serve us, not to control us. When used repetitively to suppress anxious feelings and self-doubt, habits and rituals can become superstition and compulsive obsessive disorders. Anxiety traps the individual in an elaborate ritualized behavior pattern to give a false sense of control. Re-educating your brain/body response to your key issues with the models in this book should prove helpful in handling that anxiety.

INSIGHT: My habits that mask anxiety

Are there any habits or rituals you have built into your life that you feel are masking deeper fears and anxieties? (e.g. smoking, drinking, double-checking locks or stoves)

1. _____

2. _____

At the other end of the habit spectrum, are the people who have no helpful ritual or routine to help organize their daily lives and to cope with their fears. They are therefore exhausted by the constant need to reinvent the wheel. The Fire Extinguishers can provide the nurturing rhythm and familiar structure needed for balance.

Work With Positive
Affirmations and Statements

Here is an expanded list of important affirmations that you may choose to work with in regard to your life issues. Choose the category of affirmation that seems most relevant to your issue. The affirmations on self-esteem are a good place for everyone to start, whether or not you consciously feel you need them. A Muscle Check will often reveal an imbalance around these issues of self worth.

Go through each statement one at a time. First, notice how you are impacted by the statement. Defuse it with the Emotional Stress Release technique (page 88), and Eye Rotations (page 102), or any other activities of your choosing. After you have worked with the statement, think about it again, and notice any improvements in your brain/body reaction. Read Dr. Wayne Topping's *Success Over Distress* and *Stress Release* for additional affirmations.

Fear and Anxiety (repeating the earlier section, page 105)

1. I feel safe and secure.
2. I feel calm.
3. I feel self-control.
4. I feel courage.
5. I move through my world with ease and joy.

Self-esteem

1. I like myself.
2. I love myself.
3. I love myself unconditionally.
4. I am a worthwhile person.
5. I deserve praise, admiration and respect.

Finances

1. I am successful.
2. People are happy to pay me.
3. I no longer believe it is wrong to be wealthy.
4. I no longer have to go along with limiting ideas about making and having money.
5. I deserve financial abundance.

Anti-procrastination

1. People approve of me.
2. I am successful.
3. I accept the consequences of my decisions.
4. It's OK to experience anxious feelings.
5. I complete what I start.

Success

1. I am proud of my achievements.
2. I have plenty of energy to accomplish what I want to do.
3. I have determination, drive and self-confidence.
4. I enjoy getting things done.
5. I deserve to be successful.

Goal Setting

1. I set goals easily.
2. I automatically think in a decisive and determined way.
3. I enjoy being responsible.
4. I know what I want out of life.
5. I have the power to live my dreams.

Weight Loss

1. I eat to live.
2. I believe I can lose weight.
3. I want to lose weight.
4. I like my body.
5. I am worthy of a good figure.

SECTION **9**

REFERENCE

Endnotes

SECTION 1: *The Fire of Fear Ignites:* Introduction

1.   I strongly recommend Candace Pert's book *Molecules of Emotion.* The discoverer of the opiate receptor, and a respected neuroscientist, Pert's life work is very supportive of mind/body approaches to emotional work. Pert's research supports her thesis that "Neuropeptides and their receptors join the brain, glands, and immune system in a network of communication between brain and body, probably representing the biochemical substrata of emotion" (Pert & Ruff, *Journal of Immunology*, 1985, as quoted in *Molecules of Emotion*, page 178). It seems safe to assume that this chemical information system is at work during the classic stress response, triggering the physiological changes to the endocrine, digestive, respiratory, cardiovascular, and immune systems, both a result of, and a cause of the change in emotional experience.

2.   For years surgeons have taken a muscle from one part of a patient's body and implanted it elsewhere in the body where it is functionally needed. The patient is able to retrain that muscle to perform a new function. This shows us that we can teach body cells to react in a new way. The implications are exciting: By reeducating body memory we can get better—changing cellular memory, and affecting our whole brain/body system.

3.   I have patterned my formula on the work of Three In One Concepts who language their model as Event + Perception + Intense Emotion= Fusion. Stress Release then is languaged as a "defusion" of the trauma of the past from the current event, allowing a free choice of action in the present, which in turn determines the future.

4.   This process is called myelination—the laying of a fatty protection around the established neural circuit, to prevent leakage of information, and to make transmission into action even faster. See Addenda, page 198 'Stress from the Brain's Point of View' for more insight.

5.   A brief history of Specialized Kinesiology:

The assessment tool of Muscle Checking (or testing)—isolating a muscle, and checking it for loss of function and range of motion—was first used by some medical professionals in the early 1900s. It fell into disuse with the advent of sophisticated technical diagnostic tools, and later became valued by some naturopaths and chiropractors for its natural biofeedback.

Dr. George Goodheart, a chiropractor who discovered relationships between muscle integrity, functions of the body, and meridian energy, ultimately founded the International College of Applied Kinesiology for medical professionals in the 1960s. Dr. John Thie, DC, a colleague of Dr Goodheart's, saw the need to share the basic precepts of self-care with the layperson. He combined a basic introduction to the buttons and switches of the human body with aspects of oriental meridian theory in his seminal book *Touch For Health*, first published in 1973. This started momentum for a world wide educational model of layman self responsibility that has drawn educators, healing professionals, psychologists and people from all walks of life. Many branches that have sprung from Touch For Health are collectively called Specialized Kinesiology. This book deals primarily with the stress management and performance implications of this field.

SECTION 2: *What Fires are Flaring Up?* The Pre-Check

6.   You will experience Muscle Checking later in Section 5. However, all processes in this book can be accomplished with Noticing.

7.   The concept of the role-play is integral to Educational Kinesiology, where body movement is honored as the key to learning.

8.   These lists were compiled from information offered by the Canadian Mental Health Assocation, the National Institute for Mental Health, and various other sources. They are not, nor are they intended to be, a definitive screening for Posttraumatic Stress Disorder or any other mental disorder. See a licenced mental health or medical professional for medical diagnosis. For those interested in further research, see Reference Section

9 for web pages and addresses of key associations. The Internet is a rich source of information. For additional web sites, go to any major search engine, and enter "posttraumatic stress" or "stress" for many more links.

9.   See *Making the Brain Body Connection*, pages 33–35.

10. *Science News* reports 5 minutes talking about something negative raises and maintains cortisol levels which decrease learning & memory for 5 hours. A good reason to control the classic stress response!

SECTION 3: *Fire Extinguishers:* Reeducating Your Brain/Body Response

11.   John Varun Maguire, *Become Pain Free with Touch For Health*, page 9. John generously gave me permission to source his clear explanations on energy switches. This handbook, plus his manual *Maximum Athletic Performance*, are good choices for the person interested in exploring basic Touch For Health concepts.

12.   Ibid, page 11.

13.   Ibid, page 11.

14.   In conversation with Wayne Topping, Ph.D.

15.   For simple checks for Brain Organization Profiles, see *Making the Brain Body Connection*, pages 33-35.

16.   Shannahoff-Khalsa, David, Breathing Cycle Linked to Hemispheric Dominance. *Brain Mind Bulletin*, Volume 8, Number 3, Jan. 3, 1983.

17.   Deal, Sheldon, DC, N.M.D.: *Applied Kinesiology Workshop Manual*, New Life Publishing Co., 1973.

18.   Shannahoff-Khalsa, David, Breathing Cycle Linked to Hemispheric Dominance. *Brain Mind Bulletin*, Volume 8, Number 3, Jan. 3, 1983.

19.   Craig, Gary, *Emotional Freedom Techniques: The Manual*, 1999.

21.   See "Stress from the Brain's Point of View", page 198.

20. Emotional Freedom Techniques web site allows free download of the manual—see page 221 for more information.

SECTION 4: *Checking the Embers:* The Post-Check

22. See Section 5 on pages 142–152 of this book for more in-depth information on Muscle Checking.

23. Those who are fully trained Muscle Checkers can use a Muscle Check to determine which activities would serve their brain/body most effectively.

SECTION 5: *More Fire-Fighting Equipment:* The Muscle Check

24. When one receives training in Muscle Checking, an arm muscle is usually used, in partnership with another person doing the checking. Pre-checks to assure the testing is valid are also made. Please see our Educational Opportunities section for more information.

25. If I had my wish, everyone in the world would take an introductory class in Touch For Health, which will teach them how to test for muscle performance and balance throughout the body. This is obviously a valuable step for those interested in physical performance and sports, and goes far to reeducate the body impacted by serious trauma. I equally recommend classes in Brain Gym®, Three in One Concepts, and Wellness Kinesiology, all of which build on the concepts introduced in this book. See Educational Opportunities on page 217.

SECTION 6: *Other Burning Issues:* Sources of Stress in Your Everyday Life

26. Topping, Wayne, *Success Over Distress*, page 5. Reprinted with permission.

27. This topic will be addressed in great detail in an upcoming book entitled *Making the Brain Body Connection for Success*. If you are immediately interested in more details on goal setting, see page 148 of my previous book, *Making the Brain Body Connection*. Good additional sources are *Success Over Distress* by Dr. Wayne Topping, and *Wishcraft* by Barbara Sher.

SECTION 7: *Putting Out Everyday Fires:* Applying the Model to Your Life

28. *Making the Brain Body Connection* details a 10 Step Change Process. Its emphasis is on how the brain works for enhanced learning and performance, with an exploration of sensory and fine motor integration.

29. This simple house cleaning analogy was courtesy of my colleague Cathrine Levan. It would never have occurred to me, because I have lived 27 years in the same house, with almost no cleaning of closets!

30. Adopted with permission from Edu-Kinesthetics, Inc., publishers of *Brain Gym®️ Handbook* by Paul E. Dennison and Gail E. Dennison.

31. Canadian Mental Health Association, *Coping with Stress,* 1992, pages 29–30. Reprinted with permission. See Reference Section, page 222 for contact information.

32. Hannaford, Carla, Ph.D., *Smart Moves,* 1995, pages 171–173.

33. Hannaford, Carla, Ph.D., *Smart Moves,* 1995, pages 48, 66, 90, 93, 158,171–173.

SECTION 8: Addenda

34. If you are interested in more deeply exploring the science of the stress response, I refer you to a wonderful book by Robert M. Sapolsky, *Why Zebras Don't get Ulcers.* The science is all here, leavened with witty good humor.

35. See Endnote 1. Also see Candace Pert's, *Molecules of Emotion,* pages 26-27. This is another science-based book you may find enjoyable and accessible.

36. Ibid., page 142.

37. Ibid., page 141.

Educational Opportunities

If you want to learn more about Specialized Kinesiology, contact one or more of the organizations below. As these are membership organizations, not licensing bodies, we recommend you take the responsibility of checking the experience and credentials of the instructors to whom you have been referred.

BRAIN GYM® (EDUCATIONAL KINESIOLOGY)

Brain Gym was chosen as one of 12 exemplary programs "that model excellence in the classroom and have demonstrated effective results" by a White House Task Force on Innovative Learning in Washington, DC. Originally developed to ameliorate learning challenges, Edu-K is now used internationally by educators, students, performing artists, athletes and the general public to create positive change and free movement in their lives.

> **International Educational Kinesiology Foundation**
> 1575 Spinnaker Drive, Suite 204B
> Ventura, CA 93001, USA
> phone: 800-356-2109   805-658-7942
> fax: 805-650-0524
> email: edukfd@earthlink.net
> web: www.braingym.org

THREE-IN-ONE CONCEPTS (ONE BRAIN)

More psychological in its approach, the Three-in-One Concepts model identifies on a conscious, subconscious and body level, the beliefs that have fused into old self-defeating patterns. By consciously identifying and defusing these blocks, 'One Brain' facilitates a shift in perception of our relationship with ourselves and the outer world. It allows us to respond to life with clear creative choice.

Three in One Concepts
2001 W. Magnolia Blvd.
Burbank, CA 91506-1704, USA
phone: 818-841-4786   fax: 818-841-0007
email: onebrain@earthlink.net
web: www.3in1concepts.net

TOUCH FOR HEALTH

Touch for Health is a powerful natural healing method that is the foundation upon which the Specialized Kinesiologies in this book are built. Touch for Health has proven itself very effective during the over 28 years it has been in use around the world. Using simple muscle testing, TFH shows where stress is locked into the circuits of the body. It identifies and balances these areas using techniques from acupressure, Chinese energy theory and neurolymphatic massage.

**Touch For Health Kinesiology
Association of America**
PO Box 392
New Carlisle, OH 45344-0392, USA
phone: 800-466-8342 or 937-845-3404
fax: 937-845-3909
email: admin@tfhka.org   web: www.tfhka.org

WELLNESS KINESIOLOGY

Wellness Kinesiology consists of 16 programs that teach ways to defuse stress, identify the body's nutrient needs (what it is sensitive to, and how to correct those sensitivities), as well as how to overcome addiction, decrease weight, realign the body naturally and to facilitate personal growth.

Topping International Institute, Inc.
2505 Cedarwood Avenue, Suite 3,
Bellingham, WA 98225, USA
phone: 360-647-2703   888-783-2711 (USA only)
fax: 360-647-0164
email: topping2@gte.net
web: www.wellnesskinesiology.com

ENHANCED LEARNING & INTEGRATION INC.

Professional development workshops and certificate training in all the kinesiology disciplines listed above. We custom design professional development courses and materials based on *Lightning Learning, Making the Brain Body Connection, Putting Out the Fire of Fear*, and our Facilitator Training Series. For general and booking information contact:

Enhanced Learning & Integration Inc.
#713 1489 Marine Drive,
West Vancouver, BC, V7T 1B8   CANADA
phone: 604-922-8811
fax: 604-926-1106
email: info@enhancedlearning.com
web: www.enhancedlearning.com

GENERAL ASSOCIATIONS

There are many other kinesiology models beyond the ones I have introduced in this book, some more therapeutic in nature. The membership organizations and learning institutes below can direct you to any of the above, or others that meet your needs.

Canadian Association of Specialized Kinesiology
Box 621 1926 Como Lake Avenue
Coquitlam, BC, V3J 7X8   CANADA
phone: 604-669-8481
web: www.canask.com

International Kinesiology College
Niederdorfstrasse 63,
CH-8001 Zurich, SWITZERLAND
phone: 41-1-260 46 66
fax: 41-1-260 46 63
email: kinesiology@active.ch

ASK-US Association of Specialized Kinesiologists–US
P.O. Box 147
Crownville, MD, 21032, USA
phone: 888-749-6464
web: www.ask-us.org

MORE KINESIOLOGY CONTACTS ON THE WEB

www.kinesiology.net
Excellent information on many Kinesiologies and international referrals

www.kinesiologycentral.com
Good general web site

www.touch4health.com
Web page of Dr. John Thie

www.kinesiologyinstitute.com
Web page of John Maguire

touchpointreflexology.com
Good intro to self-care

www.emofree.com/downloadEFTmanual.htm
Emotional Freedom Techniques—Excellent site on powerful energy tapping technique. Generously allows free download of 80 page beginner's manual

MENTAL HEALTH CONTACTS

Canadian Mental Health Association
970 Lawrence Ave. West
Suite #205
Toronto, Ontario, M6A 3B6   CANADA
phone: 416-789-7957
fax: 416-789-9079
web: www.cmha.ca

National Institute For Mental Health
6001 Executive Boulevard
Rm 8184, MSC9663
Bethesda, MD 20892-9663, USA
phone: 301-443-4513
fax: 301-443-42799
web: www.nimh.nih.gov

MORE WEB PAGE CONTACTS FOR MENTAL HEALTH AND STRESS RESEARCH:

www.canadian-health-network.ca

www.psych-net.org
This site has stress indicator quiz

www.adaa.org/AnxietyDisorderInfor/
index.cfm

www.cns.nyu.edu/home/ledoux/
Emotion, Stress and Memory Overview, LeDoux Laboratory, New York University

For additional web sites, go to any major search engine, and enter "posttraumatic stress" or "stress" for many more links.

Bibliography
and Recommended Reading

Other than where honoring quoted sources, books I have chosen to recommend are simple and to the point. Obviously more complex and theoretical work is available for those who feel ready for more challenging texts, but first steps first for most of us coming out of stress. Good first choices are marked with an asterisk (*).

SPECIALIZED KINESIOLOGY

Barhydt, Hap, Ph.D., & Elizabeth Barhydt: *Self Help for Stress and Pain.* Loving Life, 1989. Available through Touch For Health Kinesiology Association of America.

Callahan, Roger J., Ph.D: *Five Minute Phobia Cure; Dr. Callahan's Treatment for Fears, Phobias And Self-Sabotage.* Enterprise Publishing Inc., Wimington, DE, 1985.

Cole, Jan: *Re-Pattern Your Sabotaging Ways.* 1985. Available through Touch for Health Kinesiology Association of America.

Deal, Sheldon, DC, N.M.D.: *Applied Kinesiology Workshop Manual.* New Life Publishing Co., 1001 N. Swan Rd., Tucson, Ariz. 85711, 1973.

Dennison, Paul E., Ph.D., Gail E. Dennison and J. D. Teplitz, Ph.D.: *Brain Gym for Business.* Edu-Kinesthetics Inc., Ventura, CA, 1994.

Dennison, Paul E., Ph.D., & Gail E. Dennison: *Brain Gym Handbook*. Edu-Kinesthetics Inc., Ventura, CA, 1989.

* Dennison, Paul E., Ph.D., & Gail E. Dennison: *Brain Gym Teacher's Edition*. Edu-Kinesthetics Inc., Ventura, CA, 1989.

Eden, Donna: *Energy Medicine*. Tarcher/Putnam, New York, NY, 1999.

* Hannaford, Carla, Ph.D.: *Smart Moves; Why Learning Is Not All In Your Head*. Great Ocean Publishers, Arlington, VA, 1995.

Holdway, Ann: *Kinesiology; Muscle Testing and Energy Balancing for Health and Wellbeing*. Element, Inc., Rockport, MA, 1995.

Jeffers, Susan: *Feel the Fear and Do it Anyway*. Ballantine Books, New York, NY, 1987.

Maguire, John: *Become Pain Free With Touch For Health*. Kinesiology Institute, Malibu, CA, 1996. 1-800-501-4878 or 310-457-8407

* Promislow, Sharon: *Making the Brain Body Connection; a playful guide to releasing mental, physical and emotional blocks to success*. Enhanced Learning & Integration Inc, West Vancouver, BC, 1999.

Stokes, Gordon & Daniel Whiteside: *Improved Learning Awareness; A One Brain Text*. Three in One Concepts, Burbank, CA, 1996.

* Stokes, Gordon & Daniel Whiteside: *Tools of the Trade*. Three In One Concepts, Burbank, CA, 1996.

* Thie, John, DC: *Touch for Health*. DeVorss & Company, Marina de Rey, CA, 1973,1994.

Topping, Wayne, Ph.D.: *Stress Release*. Topping International Institute, Bellingham, WA, 1985.

* Topping, Wayne, Ph.D.: *Success Over Distress*. Topping International Institute, Bellingham, WA, 1990.

GENERAL REFERENCE

Bassett, Lucinda: *From Panic to Power; Proven Techniques To Calm Your Anxieties, Conquer Your Fears, And Put You In Control Of Your Life*. Quill, New York, NY, 2001.

Blaylock, Russell L. M.D.: *Excitotoxins; The Taste that Kills*. Health Press, Santa Fe, NM, 1994.

Bodger, Carole: *Smart Guide to Relieving Stress*. John Wiley & Sons, Inc., Toronto, ON, 1999.

Chopra, Deepak M.D.: *Quantum Healing; Exploring the Frontiers of Mind/Body Medicine*. Bantam Books, New York, NY, 1989.

Craig, G., & A. Fowlie: *Emotional Freedom Techniques; The Manual*. Self Published, The Sea Ranch, CA, 1995.

De Becker, Gavin: *Fear Less; Real Truth About Risk, Safety, and Security In A Time Of Terrorism*. Little, Brown & Co, New York, NY, 2002.

De Becker, Gavin. *The Gift of Fear; And Other Survival Signals That Protect Us From Violence*. Dell Publishing, New York, NY, 1997.

Dollemore, Doug, et al.: *Training the Body to Cure Itself; How to Use Exercise to Heal.* Rodale Press, Emmaus, PA, 1992.

Gerber, Richard, M.D.: *Vibrational Medicine. New Choices for Healing Ourselves.* Bear & Company, Santa Fe, NM, 1988.

Goleman, Daniel: *Emotional Intelligence; Why It Can Matter More Than IQ.* Bantam Books, New York, NY, 1995.

LeDoux, Joseph: *The Emotional Brain; The Mysterious Underpinnings of Emotional Life.* Simon & Schuster, New York, NY, 1996.

Miller, Jonathan: *The Human Body.* Viking Penguin, New York, NY, 1983.

* Parker, Steve: *How the Body Works.* Reader's Digest, Pleasantville, NY 1994.

* Parker, Steve: *Brain Surgery for Beginners and Other Major Operations for Minors.* The Millbrook Press, Brookfield, CN, 1993.

* Pert, Candace, Ph.D.: *Molecules of Emotion.* Scribner, New York, NY, 1997.

* Powell, Trevor: *Free Yourself from Harmful Stress.* The Reader's Digest Association (Canada) Ltd., Montreal, QUE, 1997.

Sapolsky, Robert M.: *Why Zebras Don't Get Ulcers; An Updated Guide to Stress, Stress-Related Diseases, and Coping.* W.H. Feeman & Company, New York, NY,1998.

Sher, Barbara & Annie Gottlieb: *Wishcraft; How to Get What You Really Want.* Ballantine Books, New York, NY, 1979.

Sunbeck, Deborah, Ph.D.: *Infinity Walk; Preparing Your Mind to Learn*. Jalmar Press, Torrence, CA, 1996.

* Sylwester, Robert: *A Celebration of Neurons*. Association for Supervision and Curriculum Development, Alexandria, VA, 1995.

* Van der Meer, Ron & Ad Dudink: *The Brain Pack*. Running Press, Philadelphia, PA, 1996.

Index

Achilles tendon, 122, 124
acupressure, 60, 66-67, 112, 114, 116-117
acupuncture, 67
adrenaline, 51
affirmations, 74, 103, 105, 120, 208
alarm, 20, 46-48, 53, 193
alcohol, 41, 63, 190
amygdala, 199-202, 205
anchoring, 92, 107-108, 135, 184
anxiety, 12, 19, 26, 38, 105, 122, 162, 177, 207-208
Applied Kinesiology, 21, 77, 213
Attention Deficit Disorder, 70,122, 203
auditory, 110
avoidance, 39, 102, 177
axons, 199
back brain, 46, 48, 52, 67, 87, 122, 200-202
balance, 29, 34, 46, 58, 70, 73, 76-77, 87, 114, 161, 191, 198, 215
balancers, 19, 61
Barhydt, Hap & Elizabeth, 67
basal ganglia, 70, 201
Bennett, Terrence, 60
Be Sense-Able, 110,183
biochemical stress, 160, 201, 212
biodot, 29, 238
biofeedback, 28-30, 140, 142, 146, 148, 213
brain, 10-11, 17-19, 21-22, 24-26, 28-29, 38, 45-48, 50, 52, 56-58, 62-63, 65, 67-70, 72-78, 87-91, 97-

98, 101, 103, 122, 124, 126-127, 142-150, 155, 157, 194-195, 198-204, 207-208, 214-216
amygdala, 199-202, 205
back brain, 46, 48, 52, 67, 87, 122, 200-202
basal ganglia, 70, 201
brain stem, 124, 199, 202, 204
cerebellum, 70, 122, 200-202
cerebral cortex, 98, 200-1
frontal lobe, 46,70, 87, 90, 97
hippocampus, 200-201
hypothalamus, 76
left hemisphere, 73, 76
limbic, 70
midbrain, 199, 205
reticular activating system, 70, 199-200, 205
right hemisphere, 73,76
brain/body integration, 172
brain body response, 37, 56, 136, 165, 174, 182, 187, 189, 207
Brain Buttons, 68, 184
Brain Gym, 84, 87, 112, 127, 129, 132, 184, 214-216
Brain Organization, 2, 45, 201, 214
brain hemispheres, 11, 25, 65, 69, 73-74, 110, 172
brain stem, 124, 199, 201, 204
caffeine, 63, 155, 190
Callahan, Roger, 119
Canadian Mental Health Association, 190, 215, 221
central nervous system, 22, 29, 126, 142, 146
cerebellum, 70, 122, 200-202

cerebral cortex, 98, 200-201
cerebrospinal fluid, 123, 126
change, 17-18, 48, 50, 60, 76-77, 91, 93-95, 135, 155-156, 163, 188, 212, 216
Chapman, Frank, 59
circuit lock, 18, 89, 91, 107-108, 122, 149
classic stress response, 10, 46-48, 87, 122, 156, 212-214
    alarm stage, 46-48, 53
    response stage, 46, 51
    overwhelm stage, 47, 52-53
cholesterol, 51
continuum of well-being, 155
Cook, Wayne, 80
Cook's Hook-ups, 80-83, 98, 100, 140, 183
cortisol, 51, 214
Craig, Gary, 119, 214
cross march, 25, 70-75
Cross Patterning, 25, 69, 71, 73-75, 172
circuit lock, 18, 89, 91, 107-108, 122, 149
Deal, Sheldon, 214,
Deep Breathing, 78, 190
dehydration, 62
Dennison, Paul & Gail, 5, 84, 216
digestion, 48, 119
digestive, 48-49, 87, 119, 212
distress, 36, 157, 208, 215
dominance, 76, 214
dopamine, 70
Drink Water, 24, 62-63, 140
editing a video, 93
Educational Kinesiology, 2, 5, 184, 213, 217
educational opportunities, 30, 217
electrical energy, 80

electromagnetic, 24, 60, 80, 114, 159, 194
emotion, 11, 13, 16-18, 23, 102-103, 107, 110, 143, 198-201, 212, 216, 222
Emotional Freedom Techniques, 119, 215, 221
emotional stress, 26, 87-91, 98, 115, 119, 160, 173, 193, 208
Emotional Stress Release, 26, 60, 87-91, 98, 100, 102, 105, 111
endorphins, 58, 60
Energizer, The, 2, 111, 128-129
energy switches, 22-23, 58-61, 214
    movement, 21-22, 57-58, 70, 100, 147, 201, 213, 217
    neurolymphatic reflexes, 59, 115-116, 218
    neurovascular holding points, 60, 87
    meridians, 60, 65, 67, 80, 87, 98, 117, 119-20, 213
    acupressure points, 60, 66-67, 112, 114, 116-117
    spindle cell reflex, 60, 145-146, 151, 180
Enhanced Learning, 2, 216, 219
environmental stress, 159
eustress, 157
Eye Points, 111, 114, 172, 188
Eye Rotations, 100, 103-105, 140, 188, 208
fainting, 53
fear, 9, 11-16, 19, 23, 35-36, 38, 40, 88, 91, 101, 104-

105, 119-120, 134-135, 143, 159, 162, 201-202, 208,

Fear Tapping Points, 60, 119-120, 140, 182, 188

figure 8, 80

fine motor, 216

Fire Extinguishers, 23, 34-35, 38, 56-57, 61, 92, 138-139, 149-150, 170-171, 174, 194-195, 202

Anchoring, 92, 107-108, 135, 184

Be Sense-able, 110, 183 Eye Points, 111, 114, 172, 188, Wake Up Your Ears, 112-113

Cook's Hook-ups, 80-83, 98, 100, 140, 183 Hook-ups, 84, 98, 184

Cross Patterning, 25, 69, 71, 73-75, 172, Cross March, 25, 70-75

Drink Water, 24, 62-63, 140

Emotional Stress Release, 26, 60, 87-91, 98, 100, 102, 105, 111, Touch the feeling, 95, Postural Stress Release, 96

Frontal/Occipital Holding, 97-98, 100

Energizer, The, 128-129, 140, 182, 188

Eye Rotations, 100, 103-105, 140, 188, 208, Affirmations, 74, 103, 105, 120, 208

Fear Tapping Points, 60, 119-120, 140, 182, 188

Headache Points, 115-118, 140, 182, 188

Leg Muscle Release, 124, 140, 182, 188

Neck and Shoulder Release, 130-131, 140, 182, 188

Plug In for Balanced Energy, 65-66, 140, 182, 188, Brain Buttons, 68

Polarized Breathing, 76-77, 140, 182, 188, Deep Breathing, 78, 190, Yawning, 78

Rub Out Tension and Headaches, 115-118

Sacral Spinal Pump, 126-127, 140, 182, 188

focus, 10, 30, 41, 50, 111, 114, 120, 162

frontal lobe, 46,70, 87, 90, 97

Frontal/Occipital Holding, 97-98, 100

Gall Bladder Meridian, 117

glucose, 50, 87

goal setting, 163-164, 210, 216

Goodheart, George, 59, 213

Hannaford, Carla 216, 223

hearing, 32, 44, 50, 110, 130, 187

headache, 9, 49, 115-116, 118, 140

hemisphere, 69-70, 73, 76, 201

hemispheres, 11, 25, 65, 69, 73-74, 110, 172

hippocampus, 200-201

Hook-ups, 84, 98, 184

hormones, 51-53, 126, 195, 198

hydration, 24, 62, 135, 149

hyperactivity, 122
Hyperton-X, 127
hypothalamus, 76
insulin, 50
information sandwich, 33-34, 61, 171, 174
integration, 11, 25-26, 58, 67, 75, 172, 174, 216
Insight activities, 46-47
ionization, 76
kidney, 67, 114
kinesiology, 2, 5-6, 21-22, 29, 56, 59, 77, 184, 213-215, 217-220
   Applied Kinesiology, 21, 77, 213
   Brain Gym, 84, 87, 112, 127, 129, 132, 184, 214-217
   Educational Opportunities, 30, 217
   Educational Kinesiology, 2, 5, 184, 213, 217
   Enhanced Learning, 2, 219,
   Hyperton-X, 127
   Specialized Kinesiology, 21-22, 29, 56, 212-213, 217, 220
   Three In One Concepts, 6, 69, 91, 97, 111, 124, 212, 215, 218
   Touch for Health, 6, 58, 87, 115, 119, 147, 213-215, 218
   Wellness Kinesiology, 215, 219
language development, 194
lateral, 69-70, 119
learning, 5, 47, 51, 64, 74, 129, 157, 184, 214, 216-217, 219
left hemisphere, 76

Leg Muscle Release, 124, 140, 182, 188
Levan, Cathrine, 2, 5, 215
Lightning Learning, 219
limbic system, 70
lymphatic system, 22, 59
Maguire, John, 214, 220
massage, 59-60, 66-68, 111-117, 172, 190, 217
memory, 17-18, 51, 88, 90-96, 101, 107-108, 110, 130, 200, 212-213
mental rehearsal, 90
meridians, 60, 65, 67, 80, 87, 98, 117, 119-20, 213
midbrain, 199, 204
midfield, 69
motor cortex, 200-201
movement, 21-22, 57-58, 70, 100, 147, 201, 213, 217
muscle checking, 29, 135, 142, 152, 180, 213-215
myelination, 57, 139, 212
Neck and Shoulder Release, 130, 140, 182, 188
nerves, 65
nervous system, 11, 20, 22, 29, 126, 142, 152, 198
Neuro Linguistic Programming, 21, 92, 101, 107
neurology, 17, 139
neurolymphatic reflexes, 59, 115-116, 217
neurons, 226
neurotransmitters, 70, 126, 155,198, 202
neurovascular holding points, 60, 87
noticing, 26, 30-35, 43, 46, 48, 61, 95, 140, 149, 171, 178
overwhelm stage, 47, 52-53
PACE™, 31, 68, 184

pain, 9, 18, 30-31, 39, 41, 43,
  48-49, 57, 60, 96, 99, 102,
  119, 122-123, 134, 144,
  148, 160, 214
panic, 105
perception, 16, 18, 23, 46, 218
performance, 34, 64, 147,
  214-215
Pert, Candace, 198-199, 212,
  216
physical reaction, 23, 41, 149,
  201
physical stress, 13, 16, 21, 23,
  25, 29-30, 41, 51, 63, 94,
  96, 108, 122, 149, 155-
  156, 160-162, 177, 190,
  194, 201, 215
physiology, 17, 96
Plug In for Balanced Energy,
  65-66, 140, 182, 188
polarization, 76
Polarized Breathing, 76-77,
  140, 182, 188
Positive Points, 2, 87
Post-Check, 34, 134-136, 149,
  171, 174, 185
Posttraumatic Stress, 13, 19-
  21, 38-39, 139, 213-214
Postural Stress Release, 96
posture, 17, 21, 30-31, 82, 96,
  100, 147, 159, 204
pot of stress, 158-159, 163,
  165-166, 168
Pre-Check, 27-29, 33, 135,
  171, 174, 177-178, 180
pre-checks, 35, 38, 43, 45,
  135, 150, 152, 177, 215
proprioceptors, 124, 130, 145
quadriceps, 143-145, 147-148,
  150-151, 180
Quick Six, 57, 132, 171-173
receptors, 62, 155, 199, 212

reframing, 93
repatterning, 73
response stage, 46, 51
reticular activating system,
  70, 199-200, 205
right hemisphere, 76
Ritalin, 70
ritual, 203-207
Rocker, The, 127
roleplay, 192, 213
Rub Out Tension and Head-
  aches, 115-116
Sacral Spinal Pump, 126-127,
  140, 182, 188
sacrum, 126
safety, 10, 20-21, 75, 92, 202-
  203, 204
Sapolsky, Robert M. 216,
Selye, Hans, 157
senses, 14, 46, 61, 110, 114,
  199
  hearing, 32, 44, 50, 110,
    130, 187
  proprioception, 124, 130,
    145
  smell, 40, 101, 103, 107,
    204
  taste, 40, 101, 107, 224
  touch, 25, 40, 70-72, 95,
    107, 156
  vision, 50, 78, 100-101,
    130
sensory, 11, 30, 89, 94, 130,
  157, 199, 203, 215
sleep, 84, 98, 135, 159, 191,
  193
smell, 40, 101, 103, 107, 204
Specialized Kinesiology, 21-
  22, 29, 56, 213, 217, 220
spindle cells, 60, 145-146,
  151, 180
state, 17, 20, 23, 29-30, 32-

34, 44-45, 48, 64, 80,
114, 132, 155, 171-172,
178-179, 184, 194-195,
202-205
Stokes, Gordon, 5
stomach meridian, 119-120
stress, 10-13, 18-21, 28-29, 35,
38-39, 43, 45-54, 62-63,
76, 87-91, 94, 100, 119,
122-123, 142, 144, 147,
151-159, 165-168, 173,
175-177, 190-191, 193,
195, 198, 200-202, 212-
216, 218-219
behavioral, 16-17, 35,
38-39, 42, 122, 159,
161-162, 177
biochemical, 160, 201,
212
classic stress response, 10,
46-48, 87, 122, 156,
212-213
distress, 36, 157, 208, 215
emotional, 26, 87-91, 98,
115, 119, 173, 193,
208
environmental, 159
eustress, 157
physical, 13, 16, 21, 23,
25, 29-30, 41, 51, 63,
94, 96, 108, 122, 149,
155-156, 160-162,
177, 190, 194, 201,
215
stress releaser, 24 *see also* Fire
Extinguishers
stuck circuit lock, 18, 91, 122,
149
taste, 40, 101, 107,
television, 193-194
tendon guard, 48-49, 122,
124, 199

tension, 30-31, 48-50, 61,
103, 111, 115-116, 123,
128, 130, 134, 143
tension headaches, 115
Thie, John, 6, 62, 113, 147,
213, 221
Thinking Cap, 2, 112
Three In One Concepts, 6,
69, 91, 97, 111, 124, 212,
215, 218
tombstone test, 164
toothaches, 117
Top 10 Stress Releasers, 57
Topping, Wayne, 5, 101, 208,
214-215
touch, 25, 40, 70-72, 95, 107,
156
Touch for Health, 6, 58, 87,
115, 119, 147, 213-215,
218
Touch the feeling, 95
toxicity, 52,117, 159
trauma, 10, 19-20, 38, 94, 96,
101, 110, 144, 159, 212,
215
vestibular, 70
vigilant, 20
vision, 50, 78, 100-101, 130
visual centers, 65
visual cortex, 97, 111
Wake Up Your Ears, 112-113
water, 24, 49, 59, 62-64, 100,
135, 140, 146, 149, 159,
171, 183-184
well-being, 46, 50, 57, 154-
156, 161, 194, 203
Wellness Kinesiology, 215,
219
Whiteside, Daniel, 5
yawning, 78

Train with Sharon Promislow

For those who want to master the techniques taught in this book, visit us online at www.enhancedlearning.com to arrange classes in your area. For an information pamphlet call: 604-922-8811, fax: 604-926-1106, or email us at info@enhancedlearning.com. All courses have exciting applications in the fields of education, counseling, stress management, health, creativity and sports.

Making the Brain Body Connection

Learn the science behind how your brain, body and senses interrelate, and use simple but powerful techniques to help them work better for you. Activities drawn from Specialized Kinesiology will increase sensory and fine motor co-ordination. Also included is an introduction to your Personal Brain Organization Profile, which gives a clear understanding of why we react in a predetermined way to stress. Get a clear understanding of the necessary elements for permanent change with the 10 Step Change Process. This process provides a framework to help you work through any personal issue, quickly and effectively. A practical and completely refreshing way to approach the mind-body mechanism, *Making the Brain/Body Connection* is designed and illustrated for brain-friendly reading and quick reference. Turn to product page for ordering information.

Biodots

Biodots are temperature sensitive discs that provide an instant readout of your body's thermal stress. By simple observation of the Biodot you can immediately tell when your system is reacting adversely to any given situation. When you are acclimatized to the temperature in a room the Biodot will turn green/blue if you are relaxed and alert—the ideal learning state—and lavender for a deep relaxation. It will turn black when you are under stress. Once you are aware of your stress level, you can take steps to reduce the stress by changing your environment or using the techniques you have learned in this book.

Biodots are completely safe and non-toxic. You can use them on any external part of the body but we recommend that the Biodot be placed in the web between the thumb and the forefinger on your hand. This allows high visibility for easier monitoring. See next page for ordering information.

Enhanced Learning Products

NOTE: ALL PRICES IN US DOLLARS

qty:	item:	price:
_____	*Making the Brain/Body Connection*................................	$15.95
_____	The Top Ten Stress Releasers (pad of 100)	$12.00
_____	The Top Ten Brain/Body Integrators (pad of 100)	$12.00
_____	*Putting Out the Fire of Fear*	$14.95
_____	Biodots (pkg of 10, includes shipping)	$7.95

For more information or to place an order today
FAX 604-926-1106
CALL 604-922-8811
or Email
info@enhancedlearning.com

TOTAL ORDER (USD): _____

Quantity discounts available.
Shipping/Handling not included.

Name: _____

Address: _____

City: _____ Prov/State: _____

Country: _____ Postal/Zip Code: _____

Phone: (_____) _____ Email: _____

Charge my _____**VISA** _____**Mastercard**

Card Number: _____

Exp Date: _____ Name on Card: _____

Signature _____

Mail orders please send to:
Enhanced Learning and Integration Inc.
#713 1489 Marine Drive, West Vancouver
BC, CANADA V7T 1B8

Please allow
4–6 weeks
for delivery.

About the Author

A popular speaker in the educational and public sectors and a Specialized Kinesiologist of international reputation, Sharon Promislow is a certified instructor of Stress Release, Educational Kinesiology (Brain Gym®), Touch For Health, Three In One Concepts and Brain Based Learning.

Sharon's background includes postgraduate studies in English Literature and Psychology. She was drawn to the field of Specialized Kinesiology in the 1980s by her fascination with new brain/body research and breakthroughs in learning and performance enhancement.

She is the author of *Making The Brain/Body Connection, The Top Ten Stress Releasers,* and co-authored the book *Screen Test—How to Screen for Sensitivities in Your Diet and Environment,* as well as many other professional materials. *Making the Brain/Body Connection* is one of the 100 best selling books in Cognitive Psychology, with translations in five languages.

Sharon designs and facilitates professional workshops around the world for educators, Specialized Kinesiologists and the public. She is currently developing a book series for enhancing performance in sports, the workplace and the classroom.